The New Startup
A MODERN GUIDE TO LAUNCHING A BUSINESS QUICKLY AND WITH MINIMAL COST

DAVID PIKE

Published in the United States by Acacia Books.

Library of Congress Control Number 2017919110

ISBN 978-0-9997386-0-3 paperback
ISBN 978-0-9997386-1-0 hardcover
ISBN 978-0-9997386-2-7 ebook

Printed in the United States of America

For my parents, David and Anne,
who taught me that anything is possible.

For my wife Caroline,
who has supported me in all my endeavors.

CONTENTS

Types of Businesses
Financial Status
Strengths & Weaknesses
Lifestyle
Motivation and Execution
Goal Setting

Observation
Existing Problems
Travelling
Brainstorming

Ratings, Forecasts, and Feedback
Consumer Testing – Product, Service, and
Mobile App

Customer Definition
Revenue Model
Pricing
Competitors

Introduction

Do you want to become your own boss? Are you working in a cubicle counting down the hours until 5 o'clock (or later) when you can leave the office? Are you unemployed trying to figure out what to do? Do you have a business idea but don't know where to start? Are you still searching for an idea but already know you are destined to run your own company? If any of these is the case, this book is for you. By purchasing this book, you've taken the first step to becoming an entrepreneur.

This book will provide you with a concrete step-by-step guide to starting your own business. There are many books available about entrepreneurship but they tend to be vague, outdated, and full of generic guidelines. How is this book different?

- Provides more concrete steps instead of anecdotal stories
- Introduces novel thinking and methodology including ideas such as: 1. A business plan is not a necessity; 2. Preliminary research and consumer testing is the most important factor for a business to succeed; 3. Failing isn't always a bad thing

- Highlights the latest tools you should be using including those introduced in the past year

Based on my personal experience of 10+ ventures, research from reading dozens of books on entrepreneurship, and conversations with hundreds of entrepreneurs, I will provide you with the steps and tools to start a successful business. This is the only startup book you will ever need to buy. It will teach you how to test an idea, turn it into a business with as little capital as possible, and ensure it succeeds. By following these steps, the odds of your business succeeding will exponentially increase.

Traditional jobs are no longer what they used to be. Gone are the days of spending 30 years at the same company. The current workforce tends to be more mobile; spending 2–3 years at one job, then moving on to the next. Prior to becoming an entrepreneur, I spent years in a cubicle working as a consultant. Frustrated by the lack of interesting work and the slow-moving bureaucracy of large corporations, I set out to create my own company. I wanted to work for myself while having a flexible lifestyle so I could travel around the world, have unique experiences, and meet new people. The entrepreneurial lifestyle is not for everyone. There is inherent risk involved with giving up the comfort of a 401(k) and a steady paycheck. The hours can be long, especially at the outset, but there is the opportunity to set your own hours, escape the cubicle and find a career that is more exciting and lucrative.

This book will help you launch a business with as little money as possible. When I was first contemplating entrepreneurship, I had so many ideas but did not know where to start or which idea to pursue. This book will help you generate and select the best business idea on which to launch your company. Next, it will teach you methods to de-risk your new business as much as possible to ensure that it succeeds. It will then provide you with an approach to properly structure and fund your business. Then, this book will teach you how to build a web presence, before finally laying out the best marketing strategies for your company's launch. Entrepreneurship is a journey, and you're about to take the first step. Ready? Let's start!

Chapter 1: Conduct Self-Assessment

As you embark down the entrepreneurial path, it is important to be realistic about who you are and what you want. There are many kinds of businesses you can start. Your personality and lifestyle might be more conducive to certain types of businesses than others. If you have difficulty generating business ideas, I provide a framework in the next chapter. But first here are some basic questions to ask yourself:

What type of business do you want to start?
You could consider starting a product business, a service business, or purchasing a franchise license. Product businesses include selling goods or information. You can create a new product or resell an existing product from a manufacturer. Some examples include selling clothing, selling access to a website, reselling electronics, etc. Service businesses make money by providing a service to customers. Some examples are a transportation company, business or social media consulting, dry cleaning pickup/drop-off service, etc. Some businesses, like restaurants, are a combination of service and product. You are providing customers with a service — serving of food,

preparation, cleanup, and ambience, while also providing a product (meals). A franchise is a license to sell a company's products in a particular area using that company's name. In exchange, you would pay the company a startup fee and annual licensing fees. Some franchises include McDonalds, Subway, Hertz, Ace Hardware, etc. I will not be focusing on franchises in this book as they typically require a large initial investment. My focus is on businesses you can launch quickly and effectively with low initial investment.

What is your current financial status and how much time can you commit to starting a business?
Do you have a full-time job? If so, think carefully before walking away. Strongly consider starting your first venture on the side. Don't quit until your profit covers at least 50% of your current income. The only downside of this approach is that you will have less time to spend on your business idea, and may work during lunch breaks, weeknights, and weekends. When you are starting your side venture, make sure to stay organized. Each night, create a list of tasks you want to accomplish the following day and draft emails that you can send during business hours the next day. For example, let's say you want to

email potential partners or press contacts. Draft and save the emails at night and then send them during your lunch break the following day.

Do you have $100 or $10,000 to invest in your business?

No amount is too small. In the next few chapters, I will teach you a framework which reduces how much you need to invest while also reducing risk.

What are your strengths and weaknesses?

Everyone has different strengths and weaknesses. For example, let's say you're a master at operations, but need help with your sales and marketing. You can take classes to build up your skills in those areas. Or perhaps you dislike writing. You could contract a copywriter to draft your ads and press releases There are some qualities that are critical for every entrepreneur; ask yourself if you possess them: The first is organization. Starting a business inherently involves many moving parts, and you will need to stay organized. I use an online calendar religiously to keep track of my meetings and deadlines. I'm also a strong proponent of to-do lists. Another essential quality is perseverance. There will be times when you want to give up and it seems like the odds are stacked against you. In times like these, you may need to dig deep and push on. When I was first looking for insurance for my trolley company, I approached every broker and carrier I could find. I was turned down by everyone. As I couldn't even register the vehicle without insurance, I was going to shut down the business (after I had taken out a loan and purchased the vehicle). I mentioned my problem to a friend who informed me that she had an insurance broker friend. I called up her contact, and he was able to place my policy within a few days. This experience reminded me to explore every possible avenue before giving up. Other critical traits include discipline and a strong work ethic. The hours might be long and the process of building a business can be frustrating with only a glimmer of light at the end of the tunnel, so it's important to stay focused. Overall, it's incredibly helpful to be passionate about your idea. If you are fundamentally excited about your product or service, you'll inevitably find it easier to put in long hours, maintain focus and even generate enthusiasm in other members of your team. If you don't love your product/service, how do you expect customers to love it?

Do you want the entrepreneurial lifestyle and do you have the support you need?

Financial opportunity and the freedom to set your own schedule attract many people to entrepreneurship, but there are definitely downsides; sometimes even after you are successful. Often when you start out, you will be working by yourself or with a very small team. It can be lonely. In addition, many people find the lack of structure in an entrepreneurial lifestyle difficult. You typically set your own hours, meetings, etc. which can be a big change. If you have a family, you might have more pressing financial implications and your time after work and on weekends may already be spoken for. Over time, I've come to realize how important it is to have a supportive partner and to make sure I remain social even during the more grueling initial period of a startup cycle. Discuss this situation with your spouse, significant other, or other family members well in advance to ensure they understand the sacrifices the business will require.

In addition to securing the support of your family, attempt to find strong mentors. If you know any business owners, reach out to them and ask about their experiences as an entrepreneur. Listen to their stories about the good and bad of the lifestyle. If you don't know any entrepreneurs, reach out to SCORE (www.score.org), a nationwide nonprofit that helps get small businesses off the ground. They have a vast network of entrepreneurs you can connect with. It's free and you could potentially find several mentors to help you along the way.

Achieve Success through ME — Motivation and Execution

This is one of the most important concepts in this book, so I wanted to introduce it early. Every business will fail without motivation and execution. As the owner of your own business, you need to 1) stay motivated in order to succeed, and 2) execute, because the enterprise depends on you. At the end of the day, the burden will be on you to get things done, whether it is making decisions, launching innovative marketing efforts, or making sales calls.

Along this journey, there will be days that you will lack motivation. You will want to stay in bed and watch movies. Over the years, I have found the perfect antidote for this. Keep a printout of inspirational quotes in your office. Hang the quotes in a highly visible place where you can see them. Currently, these are the quotes I have posted:

Remembering that I'll be dead soon is the most important tool I've ever encountered to help me make the big choices in life. Because almost everything — all external expectations, all pride, all fear of embarrassment or failure — these things just fall away in the face of death, leaving only what is truly important. Remembering that you are going to die is the best way I know to avoid the trap of thinking you have something to lose. You are already naked. There is no reason not to follow your heart. — Steve Jobs, Apple

Your time is limited, so don't waste it living someone else's life. Don't be trapped by dogma — which is living with the results of other people's thinking. Don't let the noise of others' opinions drown out your own inner voice. And most important, have the courage to follow your heart and intuition. They somehow already know what you truly want to become. Everything else is secondary.   Steve Jobs, Apple

Twenty years from now you will be more disappointed by the things you didn't do than by the ones you did. So throw off the bowlines. Sail away from the safe harbor. Catch the trade winds in your sails. Explore. Dream. — Mark Twain

Early to bed, early to rise, work like hell, and advertise. – Ted Turner, CNN

Life expands or contracts in direct proportion to one's courage. – Anais Nin

Scour the internet and compile a set of quotes that will keep you motivated (or feel free to borrow mine). Use your quotes as a tool to help keep focused on what you are trying to achieve for yourself.

As well as posting quotations, create a bookmarks folder on your web browser called Motivation. Find articles online that motivate you to pursue your dreams and bookmark them in your Motivation folder. Whenever you wake up and find you are lacking the energy to start conquering the day, click on one of the links in your folder. Here are the links I currently have in my Motivation folder:

www.entrepreneur.com/article/231909

www.inc.com/dan-scalco/5-billion-dollar-companies-that-were-started-as-side-businesses.html

www.businessinsider.com/richard-branson-taught-me-that-successful-people-start-before-theyre-ready-2013-8

www.entrepreneur.com/article/202258

www.forbes.com/sites/gracechung/2016/10/
05/exclusive-interview-with-one-of-americas-
most-successful-immigrants-forever-21s-do-
won-chang/

Setting Goals

One of the most important things you can do for yourself, both personally and professionally, is to set goals. Goals drive your motivation and help you focus on what's important.

Set aside 15 minutes. Take out a piece of paper, and write down 3 short-term (within a month) and 3 long-term (within a year) goals for your business. Your goals should not be vague or hazy, but concrete. They should have a measurable result and a target date to make them as concise as possible. Here are some examples:

Short-term
Form LLC by January 15th
Create list of PR contacts by January 30th

Long-term
Onboard two partnerships to sell my product by December 31st

Business will have $60k in revenue by
December 31st

Use your goals to motivate and energize you
on a daily basis. Goals should not be hidden in
a box or envelope; they are not a time capsule.
They should be displayed in a highly visible
area, around your desk or above your door, to
serve as a constant reminder. This will keep
you accountable and help you stay on track.
Your goals should be leveraged as drivers of
success.

Chapter 2: Generate Ideas

You have decided to become an entrepreneur, but you aren't sure where to start. Millions of ideas float around every day but are never realized. What separates entrepreneurs isn't the ability to generate a good idea but the passion and discipline to execute. If you are struggling to come up with an idea, don't worry. I've used the four methods below to generate hundreds:

Become more observant while living your normal daily life. As you go through your day, keep your eyes and ears open for problems. Perhaps you overhear someone complaining that the bus is running late. You could create a bus tracker app to let patrons know if there is a service disruption. Or maybe you see a stranger struggling to carry all their drone equipment. You might design a case that they can use. By remaining alert throughout the day, you will start to notice things that can be improved. Venture outside your comfort zone. Start conversations with strangers. Get a sense of what others are struggling with.

Leverage your experience of existing problems. Perhaps you are getting married and realize there are no suit rentals in your town for your groomsmen. You could create an online suit rental platform for other grooms in your situation. Or maybe you just purchased a condo and need to buy home insurance. You search online and realize there's no easy way to compare home insurance rates. You could create a website that compares rates from different insurers. Look for problems in the industry you work in. For example, you may work in advertising and realize there is a common problem all your clients are experiencing. You have a novel solution in mind which you could turn into a business.

Travel, and look for successful local businesses. Think about whether those services or products could work where you live. I call this location arbitrage. Let's say you are on vacation in New York City and see a floating barge bar on the Hudson River. Seeing how popular and successful it is, you decide to start a barge bar in Chicago on the Chicago River. I have used this method several times for my ventures. When I was travelling in Florence, Italy, I remember walking through the markets and seeing a particular item of clothing that seemed to generate a lot of sales. I began asking around to see who the manufacturer was. After speaking with the manufacturer and negotiating pricing, I quickly created a website and started running Facebook ads. Within a few hours, I had several sales. I took a product that was only available in Florence and put it online for the whole world to purchase. Another example is a coworking space I founded in Denver. On a trip to Denver, I noticed there were only a few coworking spaces available even though Denver was one of the fastest growing cities for startups. After testing the idea by putting up a website and reaching out to startups, my partner and I decided to launch the company.

Dedicate time to brainstorming. Set aside an hour with a blank piece of paper and think about different industries and problems. Let your mind wander and write down whatever comes to you. For example, you might start brainstorming about home improvement. One issue that comes to mind is finding specialty professionals like a plumber who can come to your house quickly when you need a repair. Your solution could be to create an app for on demand home service professionals (electricians, home cleaners, plumbers, carpenters, etc.). What do you like to do in your spare time? Can you turn one of your passions into a business? Let's say you love tennis. You could start a business teaching tennis lessons. Think about your passions and where there might be an unmet need. You could start a business to remedy this gap. Below are some broad areas for you to jumpstart your brainstorming:

Advertising
Art
Child-care
Clothing
Computer
Craft
Entertainment
Financial and Professional Services
Food-related
Health
Home Improvement
Lessons
Pet-related
Photography
Real Estate
Recreation
Recycling
Rental
Retail
Sports and Fitness
Technology
Transportation
Travel
Writing

Buy a small notebook and make it your Idea Book. Bring it wherever you go. Whenever you have an idea for a potential business, write it down (no matter how ridiculous). Over the next few weeks, start to fill up your notebook with ideas.

Chapter 3: Research Feasibility

Once you have 10–20 ideas in your Idea Book, review them and determine which to pursue. In my experience, most businesses don't fail because they are undercapitalized but because not enough research, testing, and preparation were done initially. In this section, you will learn to evaluate your idea, forecast potential profits, and test if consumers/businesses will even buy your product or service. By following these steps, you have a much better chance of your business succeeding.

Step 1) Determine which of your ideas already exists. You may have an amazing idea only to realize that there is another company doing exactly what you propose. The easiest way to see if your idea exists is via an online search. Let's say your idea is for a subscription gift box service for fish enthusiasts. You would search "subscription gift box service for fishing" and would see that Mystery Tackle Box already exists. That's not to say you can't start a subscription tackle box service, but my advice is to pursue an idea that doesn't have any competition yet, unless you think the competition is doing a poor job (e.g., they have a bad website, horrible customer service, or awful reviews). After you search for each of your ideas online, delete any ideas that already have robust competition.

Step 2) Rate your remaining ideas based on three attributes: investment cost, personal interest, and potential profit. Look at each idea of yours and assign three separate numbers to it based on this scale.

Investment Cost (on a scale of 1 to 10): 1 (will cost you over $2,000 to launch), 5 (costs $1,000 to launch), 10 (costs less than $200 to launch)

Personal Interest (on a scale of 1 to 10): 1 (if you're not interested at all in the idea aside from its potential profitability), 5 (you're somewhat interested), 10 (you're very passionate and excited)

Potential Profit (on a scale of 1 to 10): 1 (less than $10k in annual profit), 5 ($100k in annual profit), 10 (over $500k in annual profit)

After rating each idea with these three attributes, add up the total for each idea.

Example:

Idea	Property management	Event photography bids online	Bespoke custom clothing
Investment Cost	7	1	1
Personal Interest	1	10	5
Potential Profit	5	3	6
Total Score	13	14	12

Rank your ideas from highest total score to lowest total score. Focus on the ideas with the highest total score.

Step 3) Forecast your revenue and expenses for your top ideas. Using your forecasts, you can get a better sense of profit for each idea. Create a simple spreadsheet for each idea. On one side, estimate your revenue. On the other side, estimate your expenses. You will have both overhead and operating expenses. Overhead expenses are costs that do not change based on the quantity of products or services you sell, e.g., incorporation, insurance, internet. Operating costs are costs associated with making a product or providing a service, e.g., cost of materials, shipping.

Here is an example for a service business idea. Idea: Event planning

Revenue	Expenses
40 events per year x average fee of $1,500	Website: $200
= $60,000	Marketing: $3,000
Commission from referrals: $10,000	Conventions: $3,000
Annual Revenue: $60,000 + $10,000 = $70,000	Annual Expenses: $3,000 + $3,000 + $200 = $6,200

Here is an example for a product business idea.
Idea: Designing and selling unique tank tops

Revenue	Expenses
3,000 tank tops sold online for $20/each = $60,000	Cost of tank tops: 5,000 shirts x $5/each =$25,000
2,000 tank tops distributed to stores at $10/each = $20,000	Shopify online store: $50/month x 12 months = $600
	Payment processing fees: $60,000 x 3% = $1,800
	Marketing: $5,000
Annual Revenue: $60,000 + $20,000 = $80,000	Annual Expenses: $25,000 + $600 + $1,800 + $5,000 = $32,400

Here is an example for a mobile app idea.
Idea: Subscription service for activities in your city (ClassPass for activities)

Revenue	Expenses
Users: 1,000	Cost of building app*: $15,000
Monthly subscription price: $59	Average total user cost per month: $42
Average length of user subscription: 6 months	User lifetime cost: 1,000 x 6 x $42 = $252,000
	Marketing: $20,000
Annual Revenue: 1,000 x $59 x 6 = $354,000	Annual Expenses: $252,000 + $15,000 + $20,000 = $287,000

*To get a true sense of app development costs, search online for app development firms. Contact at least three different firms and ask for a rough estimate.

Step 4) Get feedback from family, friends, and potential customers. Pitch your ideas and see which ones they like the best. You can set up a free survey to send to your contacts (there are several free tools online). Since your friends and family might be biased, you also want to pitch to people you don't know. You should talk to potential *customers* about their needs, wants, and expectations. SurveyMonkey offers an Audience tool that lets you send a survey to a targeted panel of consumers. Here are some starter questions to ask in your survey:

<u>Identify your target demographic</u>
What is your age?
What is your gender?
Where do you live?
What is your household income?
What is your profession?
What is your education level?

<u>Assess market and pricing</u>
Would you use this service or product, and how often?
What do you like about current products or services currently on the market?
What do you dislike about current products or services currently on the market?
What concerns/questions would you have about this service or product?
How much would you pay for this service or product?

Step 5) Collectively, your rankings in Step 2, forecasts in Step 3, and feedback in Step 4, should help you identify the strongest ideas on your list. Now you can focus on your top 1–3 ideas.

Step 6) Set up consumer tests to validate your remaining idea or ideas. This step is critical and will save you money and time down the road. Before you spend all your money building an app or stocking up on inventory, make sure a significant amount of customers will pay for your product or service. You will have wasted money, time, and effort if enthusiasm expressed by family and friends doesn't correlate to market potential. Several of my ventures failed before I even started because I did not perform consumer testing. The dictum "If you build it, they will come" does not hold true in the entrepreneurial world. Based on what your business idea is (product, service, or app), there are several ways you can test it.

Product

If your business idea is for a product, create a prototype of the product. You can create the prototype yourself or hire someone in that industry to create it for you. For example, if you're planning on producing drone cases, you can buy the material yourself and create a case based on your design. Or perhaps you will be selling a unique smartphone accessory. You might need to hire someone in the industry to create a prototype to your specifications. Don't worry about producing a large quantity; you just want a few items to photograph and show to potential customers. If you are not creating a new product but rather reselling another company's product, purchase a few items (if they are not too expensive) for photographs and to show to potential customers.

Once you have received the prototype or product you are reselling, you will want to see if customers are interested in making a purchase. Below are several consumer testing methods you can employ. Select two or three to pursue.

- Use Shopify or BigCommerce to create an online storefront and start taking orders. This is a great way to test if consumers will really pay for your product. Both of these tools are very user-friendly and make it easy to set up a store. Set up a storefront, take photos of your product, and upload them to the site. Set your pricing based on similar products in the marketplace. Create a few online ads using Google AdWords (covered further in Chapter 9) to direct potential customers to your site. If you receive orders, then you know that customers will pay for your product. Refund the customer after they order if you don't have product to ship yet or be prepared to acquire product quickly.

- Launch a Kickstarter project online. Kickstarter is a funding platform for creative projects. This option has the dual benefits of both raising funds through pre-orders and building your customer base. However, it can be tough to get noticed amongst the thousands of ongoing Kickstarter projects. Plan on creating an eye-catching video so you stand out. Once your Kickstarter project is live, leverage your social network to get as much exposure as possible.

- Create an online landing page and collect email addresses of interested customers. This is an easier option than creating a full-blown online store, but it's not as effective since you cannot test if customers will actually pay for your product. You can use a service such as Unbounce to create a landing page where potential customers can enter their email address if they are interested in purchasing your product when it becomes available. You will want to run several online ads to direct potential customers to your site.

- List your product on eBay or Etsy and see if you receive any sales. This is one of the easiest ways to validate potential customers, however there are some downfalls to using either site. If your product is truly unique, users are less likely to find it on eBay since people usually search for pre-existing products. Etsy has strict product guidelines and may not target the right customers for your product. Once again, refund the customer after they order if you don't have product to ship yet or be prepared to acquire product quickly.

- Visit retail stores in your area that sell products with the same scope as yours. Ask for the buyer (generally the manager in smaller stores) and pitch your product. Before you enter any store, make sure you know what your cost per item will be and what your wholesale price to the store would be. The store will markup your product to the retail price. Markup percentages vary by product and industry. For example, a shirt may cost a manufacturer $5 to produce. The manufacturer would sell the shirt to a store for $10 (wholesale price). The store would then sell the shirt to a customer for $20 (retail price).

- Email and call retail stores outside of where you live about selling your product. Your goal is to see if stores are interested in stocking your product. Below is a sample email template you can use:

Hello *buyer first name,*
I love *store name* and appreciate *list what you like about their store*. My name is *your name* of *your company name*. I've been receiving calls from customers in your area who are looking for a local store to buy our product. We produce *your product name*. Our product is unique and I believe will fly off your shelves. I can offer competitive wholesale pricing and low minimum order quantities. I've attached product images to this email. Please reach out to me with your thoughts. I would love to set up a phone call to discuss further.

Thank you for your consideration and I look forward to hearing from you!

Best,
your name
your company name

If you don't hear back from the buyer, follow up every few weeks. If you hear back and the answer is no, don't give up hope yet. Reach out to the buyer again and say that you believe in the product so much, that the buyer can offer it on consignment. Consignment is where retailers will stock your product but will not prepay you for inventory. They will pay you only if they sell your item to a customer. Consignment provides retail stores with a low-risk option to test your product.

Service
If your business idea is for a service, you need to assess whether potential customers are interested in using your service. You can achieve this by using one or several of the following methods:

- Create a website and start taking bookings. Using an online website builder, create a simple website with the goal of receiving customer inquiries via phone or email. Building a website is easy and can be finished in as little as a few hours, even if you are less comfortable with technology. I will guide you through the process of building a website in Chapter 8. After you launch the website, you will want to run online ads using Google AdWords to direct users to your site. Overall, this process takes several hours and will cost you about $100. It is well worth the investment since it will help you determine if people will use your service.

- In place of creating a full website, you could create a simple landing page and collect email addresses of interested customers using a service such as Unbounce or Lander. Once again, you will want to run online ads using Google AdWords to direct users to your site.

- Call and email potential customers to see if they would be interested in using your service. Let's say you are starting a social media consulting firm. You could call local small businesses and describe your offering and pricing. Convince them to commit to your service. Post online to special interest forums related to your product or service. Ask members for feedback and gauge their interest in becoming customers. Think outside the box about ways you can reach potential customers and then execute.

Mobile App

If your idea is mobile app-based, create a single page website or landing page detailing what the app does and its benefits. You can indicate "Coming Soon to App Store" and "Coming Soon to Google Play" on the homepage. Let's say you are creating an app for consumers that provides restaurant deals on certain weeknights. You would create a website detailing benefits of the service and state "Our app is under development and will be available in *future month/year*." Include a field on your website to capture email addresses of interested customers. You could entice visitors to provide their email address by saying that you will be providing free trial memberships to those who sign up during the pre-launch phase. You should run a few online ads to direct people to your website. If people start signing up for your service and your email database grows, that's a reliable indicator that consumers are interested in your app.

Tip: When applying these testing methods, you want to "build a Hollywood set" — the façade looks great but there's no piping inside. You want to present your business as if it is already established to get a true sense of consumer interest.

Once you've tested your ideas using the above methods, you should have a sense of whether customers are interested in your product or service and know whether or not it's worth pursuing. It's hard to walk away from an idea, especially if you are excited by it, but your time and money are important, and you don't want to waste them. Start generating more ideas and repeat the testing methods you've learned. Eventually, you will find an idea that generates enough consumer interest to warrant starting a business around it. If you have found an idea that customers are excited about, you are ready to move on to the next step — defining your product or service.

Chapter 4: Define your Product/Service

If the consumer tests of your idea went well and you generated interest from potential customers, you are ready to start your company! If the consumer test did not go as planned, do not give up. Start thinking of more ideas and repeat the steps you just learned. I've had more ideas fail at this stage than come to fruition, and it's all part of the process.

Once the idea has been validated, it's time to further define your product or service. Should you write a business plan? No! Business plans are outdated documents. People spend months creating a business plan and never look at it again once it's finished. After you launch your business, all your preconceived notions about your company might — and probably will — be wrong. You may believe that your customers will be one segment only to realize that you are selling to a completely different customer segment. In my trolley company, I assumed my customers would be 22–30-year-olds celebrating birthdays and happy hours. A few months after launching, I realized that 70% of my business was from brides for their weddings. Even though you do not have to write a business plan, you will still want to answer several critical questions about your business.

What is your product or service?
Write one sentence describing what your business provides.

Who is your target customer?
Define who will be buying your product or using your service. Be specific about their age, gender, interests, and where they live.

What is your revenue model and sales strategy?
Are you selling to consumers or businesses? Which revenue model are you using? There are several types of revenue models:

Ad-based — make money off ads on high-traffic websites or apps (example: CNN.com)

Affiliate — promoting links to products and collecting commissions

Transactional — customer pays directly for service or product

Web Sales — customer pays directly for service or product and conducts transaction solely over the internet (example: Amazon.com)

Retail Sales — setting up a traditional retail store to sell your physical goods to a customer

Channel Sales — having your product or service sold through a third-party partner or reseller

Subscription — recurring monthly or annual revenue (example: gym membership)

Freemium — product/service are free, but customers must pay for more features (example: LinkedIn)

What is your pricing?
Determine how much you will charge for your product/service.

What are your costs?
Define what your overhead and operating costs will be.

Who are your competitors?
Determine your direct and indirect competitors. Direct competitors are companies that have a very similar product/service as an alternative to yours. Indirect competitors are businesses offering different products/services but target the same group of customers to

satisfy the same need. For example, gym memberships, fitness equipment sales, and diet programs are all indirect competitors of each other as they are all targeting customers interested in weight loss.

Here are some examples to get you started.

Example A
What is your product or service? My company sells unique tank tops depicting popular internet memes.

Who is your target customer? Males/females worldwide; ages 18–40; interests include concerts, travel, and fashion.

What is your revenue model and sales strategy? My company sells the shirts directly to consumers online (company website and Amazon) as well as wholesales the shirts to retailers across the country. If retailers will not stock the product initially, we will pitch consignment to them.

What is your pricing? $25–$30 retail per shirt; $10 wholesale to retailers.

What are your costs? My operating costs are the cost of the shirt ($4/each) and the printing cost ($1/shirt). My overhead costs include website hosting ($15/month), email ($5/month), and marketing ($150/month).

Who are your competitors? There are many online shops that sell tank tops, but my company has unique designs that no other company is offering.

Example B
What is your product or service? My company provides a website that allows users to compare home insurance rates.
Who is your target customer? Recent homeowners and homeowners renewing their annual home insurance policy in the U.S.

What is your revenue model and sales strategy? My company offers free quote comparison for consumers via an online portal. We plan to partner with other sites targeted towards homeownership (e.g., bankrate.com). Once we have enough web traffic, our revenue will be earned from two sources: ads that consumers click on and commissions from insurers (for providing customer leads).

What is your pricing? Pricing is free for consumers.

What are your costs? My overhead costs are the cost of the developer to build this complex website ($4,000), website hosting ($15/month), email ($5/month), and marketing ($150/month).

Who are your competitors? There are a few companies that claim to do this, but upon entering your personal information online, you don't receive a quote. These websites just collect your personal information and send it to home insurers.

After you've answered these critical questions, it's time to structure your business.

Chapter 5: Structure the Business

You've decided what your company is going to do and formulated your overall strategy. Now it's time to complete a checklist of necessary tasks to set up your company.

1) Name your business
You want to have a unique name that consumers will remember. Your business does not have to share a name with your product. It can be an umbrella name for your company. This can be helpful in case you expand to other products or services, so you won't have to rename your company. For example, you might sell a unique product called Dog Cleansing Wash. Let's say down the road you start to sell a Cat Cleansing Wash, so it would behoove you to name your company Pet Soaps.

a) Brainstorm until you have a list of 5–10 company names.

b) Search online to see if there is a company or website that already uses that name. You will confuse potential customers if there are two companies named Tony's Lawn Care.

c) Check with your secretary of state to see if there is a business already using that name. For most states, you can do this online. Refer to Appendix C for Secretary of State contact information for each state.

d) If after your research, you still have several potential names, test them out with friends and family to see which one they like the best. Once you have decided on a name for your business, you are ready for the next step.

2) Buy a domain name, set up email addresses, and set up your business phone

After you decide on a business name, you need to register a domain for your website. You will want a unique and memorable domain name (the shorter the better). If your business name is long, you will want to use a condensed domain name. For example, if your business name is Tony's Lawn Care Service, don't use www.tonyslawncareservice.com. Instead, use www.tonyslawncare.com.

Strongly consider using .com since it is more professional than other domain extensions such as .biz, .co, and .info. Search online to make sure your preferred domain name is available. Here is one of the many sites you can use to search for available domain names. www.instantdomainsearch.com

There are many domain registrars from which you can choose. Besides selling domain names, some registrars also sell mailboxes (email addresses) and include website builders. The largest combined domain registrars, web hosting, and website builder companies are Squarespace, Wix, and Weebly. I've found it easier to keep your domain name, website hosting, and mailbox billing all in one place. A domain will cost about $15/year and one mailbox costs $5/month (through Google's G Suite). Once you buy your domain name, you should buy email addresses associated with it. When starting out, I would buy just one mailbox for your domain either _info@yourdomain.com_ or _yourfirstname@yourdomain.com_.

It's also important to have a business phone number to increase the impression of professionalism. You could consider using your personal number but having a separate business line is preferable. Google Voice is free and allows you to have a second phone number that Google assigns to your cell phone. This second number will serve as your business phone number. Download the Google Voice app to your smartphone and use it to call customers, partners, and vendors.

3) Incorporate your business

You need to form a legal entity to protect your personal assets from business debts and liabilities. Forming a legal entity also provides you with additional credibility and legitimacy. The most common options for legal entities are limited liability companies (LLCs), S corporations, and C corporations.

LLCs are often the best option for small businesses. The benefits of an LLC include reduced paperwork, less stringent reporting, and a more flexible management structure. Also since LLCs are flow-through entities (business income/loss is passed through to the owner's tax return each year), it makes tax time much easier. With LLCs, you do not take a salary since all income flows directly through your tax return. This is how you pay yourself from the company.

If you are planning to take outside investment,

forming a corporation makes more sense. Corporations provide an easier vehicle for outside investors to invest in your company. If you decide to go this route, you have two options—an S corporation or C corporation. S corporations are more closely related to LLCs in that they are flow-through entities. In S corporations, the number of shareholders (individuals who own stock in a corporation) is capped at one hundred, and shareholders must be U.S. citizens or resident aliens. In C corporations, you can have as many shareholders as you want, and there are no restrictions on their citizenship. However, C corporations are not flow-through entities, so the business must pay corporate income tax. To avoid double taxation at the end of the year, you will want to pay yourself a salary throughout the year.

After deciding upon a legal entity, you can create the entity independently using your secretary of state's website or you can use a service, which adds minimal cost. Some services that form LLCs and corporations online are legalzoom.com, corpnet.com, mycorporation.com, bizfilings.com, and rocketlawyer.com. Formation fees vary by state and can range from $50 to $500. Some people argue that you should form your LLC or corporation in Nevada or Delaware regardless of where you live since they have more business-friendly laws and tax treatment. I am a proponent of incorporating your company in the state in which you live. By doing this, you can avoid having to pay a registered agent in a different state to receive and forward your mail to you.

4) Apply for an Employer Identification Number (EIN) online

After you form an LLC or corporation, apply online for an EIN from the IRS at the website below.

www.irs.gov/businesses/small-businesses-self-employed/apply-for-an-employer-identification-number-ein-online

The EIN is mandatory since you need it to report taxes, open a business checking account, and apply for licenses. After applying online, you will receive the EIN instantly on the confirmation screen.

5) Obtain licenses/permits

What licenses and permits do you need to operate your business? Depending on the type of business you start, there may be licenses required at the federal, state, county, and city level. Research which permits and licenses you need. For the federal level, here is a good place to start:

www.sba.gov/business-guide/launch/apply-for-licenses-permits-federal-state

For the state level, reach out to your state's business licensing department. For the city level, check with your city's business affairs office. Let's say you are starting a taco truck. You will probably need a food truck operating permit. Or perhaps you are launching a pet grooming service. You may need an animal care permit.

6) Open a business checking account
Once you have your LLC/corporation filing receipt and EIN, go to a bank branch and open a business checking account. For simplicity, I would use the bank where your personal account is. This way you can have both your personal and business accounts on your online portal. In addition, many banks offer promotions and reduced fees for having multiple account relationships at one bank. Often larger nationwide banks such as Chase, Bank of America, Wells Fargo, etc. are a better choice. They offer more features on their online portals including easy account transfers and

online payroll services for contractors and employees.

7) Apply for a business credit card

After you've opened a business checking account, you will want to apply for a business credit card. You can use your business debit card to cover initial expenses, but eventually you will want to start building your business credit for several reasons. First, it will make it easier to find financing down the road. Second, businesses have 10 to 100 times greater credit capacity compared to personal credit. Third, building your credit increases the value of your company. If you eventually sell the company, business credit transfers to the new buyer. Last, you protect your personal credit. By avoiding commingling your personal and business credit, you protect yourself in case the business fails. Which business credit card should you choose? There are a plethora of options. I typically choose credit cards with cash-back rewards. Search online to compare options. You can start by browsing www.creditcards.com/business.php.

8) Create a logo and business cards

A company logo helps you build your brand. You can create a logo yourself or hire a designer. If you create a logo yourself, consider using www.freelogodesign.org so you have a more professional-looking logo. If you would like to hire a designer, you can search online for a designer or use sites such as www.fiverr.com and www.99designs.com to source logo designers.

Once you have a logo, you will want to order business cards. There are dozens of companies you can find by searching online. In the past, I've used www.vistaprint.com for my business cards. They have great quality and low prices. You will want your business cards to include your logo, company name, website, your name, title (optional), business phone number, and email address. You want your business cards to stand out from others. Imagine going to a networking event and receiving dozens of business cards. Which one would you remember? The plain black and white one or the one shaped like a rocket ship? Consider changing the stock and shape of the paper, or using a unique color set. This will increase your cost for the cards, but will be well worth it.

9) Find office space

When starting your business, you have several options for a workspace. The easiest option is to work from home, whether at a desk in your bedroom, the kitchen table, or a dedicated home office. However, if you get distracted easily and find yourself unable to get work done, you might need a different environment. Another low-cost option is to work at a coffee shop or public library. With strong Wi-Fi and a more social atmosphere, these places can be great workspaces for entrepreneurs and serve as a meeting location for customers and clients. If you are willing to pay a bit, you could sign up for a coworking space if your city has one available. One of the largest coworking spaces is WeWork, which is currently in 50+ cities. They provide you with fresh coffee, a desk, Wi-Fi, access to conferences rooms, and even some networking events. Prices range from $100–$400 per month. One of the biggest benefits of coworking spaces is the networking opportunities it provides with other like-minded entrepreneurs. You could find partnerships or even a co-founder in these spaces. Consider working from home initially in order to save money, then as you start to earn revenue, you can begin to look at coworking spaces.

You also need a mailing address for your business. The easiest option is to use your home address but this has the potential to appear less professional. If you are at a coworking space, you could use their address; note that if you were to change office spaces, you would need to update your address for everything (bank account, credit card, LLC/corporation filings, government licensing agencies, etc.). You could also use a virtual office for your business mailing address. Virtual offices provide you with an address for your business and perform mail receiving and forwarding. They are an inexpensive option and available in many cities across the U.S. Do not use a P.O. Box for your business address. It looks sketchy and UPS/FedEx will not deliver to P.O. Boxes.

10) Determine if you need a co-founder

Bringing on a co-founder may make sense in certain situations. If you lack certain skill sets that are critical for your business, having a co-founder can be beneficial. Or, if you are applying to an accelerator (covered in the next chapter), many like to see two founders on the application. Think about your skill sets and how they relate to your business. Are there critical skill sets that are missing in your business? Every business is different. You might need a tech co-founder, a marketing co-founder, or even a medical co-founder.

Let's say your business requires a complex

website and you don't have a programming background. It might make sense for you to bring on a technical co-founder. To find a tech co-founder, you have several options. You can look for developers who are mutual connections among your friends. This is preferable as it will be a friend of someone you know. You can also attend tech events in your community and network with developers. Or you can search online at techcofounder.com. They are a pairing service for founders on both the technical and business side.

In return for your co-founder's participation, you would offer him/her equity in your company. Make sure your co-founder's equity builds over time based on hitting certain targets you set. You don't want to offer 30% of your company on Day 1. Also, make sure your co-founder is financially invested in the business since you want him/her to have some skin in the game. Before bringing on a partner, spend a good deal of time with him/her and make sure that you gel; you are about to engage in a potentially long-term relationship and want to make sure he or she is the right fit for you and your company.

Chapter 6: Fund your Company

Will you self-fund and bootstrap? Will you take investment from others? There are several ways to fund your business from self-funding to debt to equity financing. The first step is to estimate how much money is necessary in the first 6–12 months. Look at your cost estimates you made in Chapter 3 and further refine them to get a sense of how much capital you will need. Through my experiences, I have created a preferred funding hierarchy. The first funding option on the list (free grants) is the most preferable and the last funding option (family and friends) is the least preferable since I don't feel comfortable risking friends' and family's money. Start at the top of the list and work your way down until you have the funds you need.

1. Apply for free grants. Grants are funds received as gifts that you do not have to repay. Many government entities provide grants from the federal level to state and regional levels. Some corporations provide grants as well as organizations focused on funding specific communities. Grants are competitive, so make sure your business is appropriate and prepare a strong application. Here are some links to help you search for grants.

Federal Small Business Grants

www.grants.gov —
comprehensive database of grants
administered by various government agencies

www.business.usa.gov —
uses a questionnaire to help you find relevant
grants

www.sbir.gov/sbirsearch/solicitation/current
— grants for technology innovation and
scientific research

www.challenge.gov —
lists government grant competitions

www.grantwatch.com —
lists grants for small businesses, nonprofits,
and individuals

State and Regional Small Business Grants

www.sba.gov/tools/local-assistance/sbdc —
provides you with a list of local Small Business
Development Centers that you can contact to
find grant opportunities

Corporate Small Business Grants

www.smallbusinessgrant.fedex.com—
FedEx small business grant up to $25,000

www.mltapthefuture.com —
live pitch competition for grants from$20,000-
$100,000

www.nase.org/become-a-member/grants-
and-scholarships/BusinessDevelopmentGrants
.aspx —
offers monthly $4,000 grants to small
businesses

Specialty Small Business Grants
For Women —
www.entrepreneur.com/article/290807

For Veterans —
www.nerdwallet.com/blog/small-
business/small-business-grants-for-veterans

For Minorities —
www.nerdwallet.com/blog/small-
business/small-business-grants-minorities

Once you determine the grants you will apply
to, you are ready to write your proposal. Grant
writing is an art. Thoroughly research the
funding organizations so you can better tailor
your proposal. Your goal is to create a
compelling and well-organized narrative for
your reader.

2. If your business sells a unique product, consider using a crowdfunding site like Kickstarter or Indiegogo. This allows you to take customer pre-orders and receive funding for manufacturing inventory.

3. Apply to accelerators. Accelerators are highly competitive programs designed to help entrepreneurs succeed. An accelerator generally provides your company with funding (typically $20k-$100k), guidance, and connections. In return, they take a percentage of equity in your company (typically 5%-10%). You would have to move to where the accelerator is located for the length of the program (typically 3-6 months). You would join a community of other startups in the program, be provided with networking opportunities, and have the chance to elicit feedback from your peers. If you are comfortable with giving up some of your equity, definitely consider applying to accelerators. Be aware that accelerators are competitive, so carefully prepare a strong application. As an example, Y Combinator has an acceptance rate of less than 2%. In addition, many accelerators like to see two founders on their application, so you may have to consider bringing on a partner. Here are some of the biggest accelerators to check out:

Ycombinator.com
Angelpad.org
Techstars.com
Amplify.la
Startx.com
500.co
F6s.com/accelerators (search tool for accelerators)

4. Obtain funding from an angel investor. Angel investors are wealthy individuals looking to put seed money into a venture. Pitching to an angel investor is a great way to validate your business, and there are many angel investor groups across the world. In exchange for providing you with funding, angel investors will take an equity position in your company. The downside of using an angel investor is that you lose some control, as the angel investor will more than likely take an active role in decision-making for the company. Search online for groups located in your city or state. Here are some sites and groups to get you started:

Angelcapitalassociation.org/directory
Gust.com
Angel.co
Startupangels.com

Allianceofangels.com
Goldenseeds.com/angel-network

5. Self-fund your startup. Review your personal finances and see how much you can afford to contribute to your startup. Don't mortgage your house, but maybe you have money in a savings account that you could leverage for funding. 57% of startups are self-funded[1]. Your individual preference may vary between self-funding or using an accelerator/angel investor. If you are not comfortable giving up equity, then you should try self-funding first. However, if you want to de-risk your investment as much as possible, use an accelerator or angel investment before self-funding.

6. Apply for a bank loan for your business. Traditional bank loans will be more difficult to obtain since your startup does not have any history, assets, or revenue. However, most banks can offer you U.S. Small Business Administration (SBA) loans. This means that your lender will be protected if the business fails since the SBA will pay a portion of the loan back to the lender. This benefits you since the lender is more likely to provide you with a

---

[1] https://www.entrepreneur.com/article/230011

loan. There are several SBA loan programs but the two most common for startups are 7(a) loans and microloans. The vast majority of startups use 7(a) loans since they can be used for a wide variety of business purposes including working capital, equipment purchases, refinancing debt, buying a business, and buying commercial real estate. The maximum loan amount is $5 million, and the repayment terms can be up to 10 years for working capital and 25 years for commercial real estate. The drawback of the 7(a) program is that the application process can take months.

For a quicker option, consider SBA Express loans under the 7(a) program which take a few days for an approval decision. The maximum loan amount on an SBA Express loan is $350,000. Even smaller than Express loans are SBA Microloans. Their maximum loan amount is $50,000 and the loan can only be used towards working capital, not real estate. Their maximum repayment term is six years. The interest rates of SBA loans vary based on credit score, loan size, repayment schedule, and current market interest rates. To apply for an SBA loan, visit your bank and ask about different loan options, or you can use the SBA's Lender Match tool at sba.gov/lendermatch.

Consider taking out a bank loan only if you're using it to purchase a hard asset that you can sell if the business fails. Hard assets include vehicles, buildings, and machinery. I would not seek a business loan if you are using it to build a soft asset like a website or mobile app since there is no resale value if the business fails.

7. Seek money from family and friends. I use this as a last resort since I don't feel comfortable with the risk of losing my friends' and family's money. Also, mixing family and friends with business can strain the relationship if the business fails. However, sometimes this is the only way to get your venture off the ground. If you choose this option, make sure to make it official by writing out and documenting the loan. Communicate progress regularly to demonstrate professionalism and show you are taking their involvement seriously.

You may have noticed that I did not include credit cards or venture capital on the list. Financing your startup using credit cards is a risky proposition for an entrepreneur. Interest rates are higher in the long-term, and you will be personally responsible for any debt if the business fails. As for venture capital firms, they rarely invest in early-stage companies. They need to see traction, customers, and growth. Venture capital funding will be covered later in Chapter 11 "Scale the Business."

Chapter 7: Prepare your Operations

It's time to discuss how to run your business on a day-to-day basis. Is your business a product company or service company? This will determine what kind of foundation you need to build your business. How will you accept payments? Do you need to hire contractors? What about insurance or trademarks? How should you manage bookkeeping? These are some of the important questions you need to answer to codify your business operations, and we will address them one by one.

Product Company

If you are selling a product, there are critical questions you need to answer:

Where will you get your products?

1. If you creating a new or custom product, you can:

> A) Create the goods yourself. If you've created a product and can manufacture it yourself, this is a low-risk and low-cost option until you need to expand. You can create more product as you receive orders, and you don't have to hold that much

inventory. Let's say you have started a t-shirt company. Prior to launching, you could purchase a heat press and limited quantities of solid color t-shirts. When orders come in, you could create the customers' t-shirts as needed. Your initial investment would be limited to the cost of the heat press and a few shirts.

B) Use a local manufacturer. You could find a small factory in the U.S. to produce your product. This offers significant advantages including a higher level of control over your product, faster shipping times, and the ability to avoid language barriers, time zone barriers, and customs/importation taxes. However, domestic manufacturers are typically more expensive than sourcing your product from abroad. To find a local manufacturer, search online based on your product type, attend a trade show in your product's industry, or leverage an online directory such as Kompass, Maker's Row, or ThomasNet. You want to find a manufacturer that has knowledge and experience related to your product. Find out their minimum order quantity (MOQ) and turnaround times. Reach out to several factories for quotes and ask them to replicate your product. Make a decision based on the quality of the product, cost, MOQ, and production timeline.

C) Use an international manufacturer. International manufacturers, particularly in countries such as China or India, often offer a very cost-effective solution. However you are more likely to encounter communication issues with the factory, import/product regulations, and delays. To find a manufacturer, you can attend a trade show in your product's industry or you can search an online directory. Some directories include Alibaba, Indiamart, Bambify, Global Sources, and Kompass. Search for manufacturers that sell items in your niche. Reach out to them and ask them if they can produce your product, price per item, and minimum order quantity. Narrow your search down to three manufacturers. Send each of them a sample of your product, have them replicate it, and send it to you for approval. Compare the quality of the replicated product from the three manufacturers. Taking into consideration the price and minimum order quantity, determine which manufacturer you would like to produce your product. You will have to take into account the added cost of using a customs broker, import taxes, and higher international shipping costs, so an international manufacturer might make sense only if you are producing a significant quantity of items. In one of my ventures, I was importing clothing from Italy and paying $5 per item excluding shipping and customs. I contacted three Chinese suppliers on Alibaba and sent them samples. One supplier was able to duplicate the item with better quality than the other two. I chose this supplier and paid $1.85 per item excluding shipping and customs, a savings of 63% over my previous supplier in Italy.

2. If you are reselling another company's products, you can:

A) Consider dropshipping. With dropshipping, you do not have to buy or hold any inventory. You would list other companies' products on your website, and when you receive a customer order, that company would ship directly to your customer. For example, let's say you've created an online store that sells home fitness equipment. Your site offers a massive selection of equipment from several different wholesalers. Instead of purchasing the equipment in advance and storing it in your home or warehouse, the wholesaler would ship the item directly to your customer when you receive an order on your website. You would only have to pay for the item when the wholesaler ships it. There is no upfront investment necessary since you don't have to pay for inventory in advance. Despite much lower risk, the downsides are that customer service may suffer (since you don't control shipping) and you will make less profit. Manufacturers offer less of a discount for dropshipping vs. if you bought a large quantity of items in advance and stored them yourself. To start a dropshipping business, find products you want to sell and reach out to manufacturers and wholesalers to see if they offer dropshipping.

B) Purchase items wholesale. You could buy products in bulk from manufacturers or distributors. By buying in bulk, you will receive a better price per item. However, the first drawback is that you will have to store those items. Second, you have the potential for excess inventory risk. Perhaps you order too much inventory and your items aren't selling quickly. You could be sitting on your inventory for a long time. To de-risk your business, consider purchasing a small amount of inventory initially even though you will pay a higher price per item. It's tough to accurately predict initial customer demand, and you don't want to be sitting on stock that no one wants. As sales increase, you can purchase more inventory. Make sure to monitor your inventory closely so you know when to reorder if your stock gets low. You don't want to be flooded with customer orders only to find that you have two items left in stock.

C) Purchase products at auctions. You could buy products at a steeply discounted price at government and private auctions. These products can come from manufacturer surpluses, business liquidations, and government dispositions. You can find auctions online for any type of product from cars to electronics to clothing. Some sites include liquidation.com, palletbid.com, techliquidators.com, gsaauctions.gov, and govsales.gov.

Where will you store your products?
To fulfill customer orders, you will need to have products on hand or readily accessible. There are several options when it comes to

storing your products:

A) Store your products at home. This is the easiest and cheapest option and might be the best route initially. Let's say you create a website selling smartphone camera accessories. You decide to purchase 200 accessories from a factory in China. Since the accessories are small, you can store them at home. When customer orders arrive, you fulfill the order yourself.

B) Store with a third party order fulfillment company. If you are selling your items on Amazon, you can have Amazon store your items for you and ship when they receive an order. Another option for storing and shipping your inventory is Shipwire. Shipwire has warehouses all across the country to store inventory. After integrating your website with Shipwire, they will automatically fulfill and ship customer orders for you when they arrive. By using Amazon or Shipwire, you will pay a bit more for storing/shipping inventory but it will save you time since you don't have to ship the orders yourself. If you have a generous profit margin, this option might make sense.

C) Store at a warehouse or storage unit. If you don't have enough room at home and don't want to use an order fulfillment company, then you will have to pay for space at a storage unit or warehouse. Whenever you receive an order, you will have to visit the storage unit/warehouse, pick up the item, and ship yourself. If you are selling large items, this option might make sense.

How will you ship your products?
If you are using an order fulfillment company or dropshipping, you don't have to worry about shipping. However if you are storing inventory yourself, then you will have to ship items when customer orders arrive.

If the size of your product is small (e.g., t-shirts, electronic accessories), consider using a home shipping/postage service like Stamps.com. They allow you to ship from home so you don't have to visit the post office. After you sign up, they mail you a free scale and provide you with software to print out labels. When customer orders arrive, you package the item, print a shipping label, and drop inside your local mailbox.

If your product is larger or heavier, you will

want to create a small business account with UPS or FedEx. By creating an account, they will provide you with discounts and the ability to print out labels from home. When you need to ship an item, you can either drop the package at a UPS/FedEx location or schedule a pickup.

Service Company
If you've started a service business, your purchase needs will vary based on your type of business. What equipment do you need to operate your business? If your service is knowledge (e.g., consulting and advisory companies), then you don't have big capital expenditures on equipment. However if you are starting a food truck or transportation business, then you will need to buy or lease a vehicle. Based on what your business does, research online to see what equipment, machinery, or tools you will need to operate. If the equipment is expensive, try leasing instead of buying. Let's say you are starting a cupcake company. As you start to scale beyond your home kitchen, you could lease space from a commercial kitchen for your baking needs. Or perhaps you are starting a dry cleaning pickup and delivery service. You could lease a van from a manufacturer or consider a timeshare with individuals or other businesses who own

vans.

Accepting Payment

Prior to launching your business, you will need to determine how you will accept payment from customers. You can accept payment in person, on the phone, or online. Consider only taking payment online as this is the easiest and least time-consuming method for you and your customers. Below are example payment options.

In person—cash; checks; credit/debit cards through Square or PayPal

On the phone—credit/debit cards through Square or PayPal

Online—PayPal balance; credit/debit cards through Stripe, PayPal, or Authorize.net

Square—Square processes credit and debit cards using a smartphone attachment and their mobile app. You can either swipe a customer's credit card in person or manually key in a customer's credit card if they are not present. Square charges a fee of between 2.75% and 3.5% + $0.15 per transaction depending on which method you use. The funds are automatically deposited into your bank account within 1–2 business days. Account sign-up is free, and they mail you the smartphone attachment at no cost.

PayPal — Like Square, you can use PayPal's mobile card reader to accept credit and debit cards from customers. You can also key in customer card numbers. Their fee is between 2.75% and 3.5% + $0.30 per transaction depending on which method you use. In addition, you can integrate PayPal with your website so customers can check out online. Customers have the option of paying with their PayPal balance or a credit/debit card. The fee for this processing is 2.9% + $0.30 per transaction. After a customer checks out using PayPal, money is deposited into your PayPal account. However, you can direct PayPal to automatically transfer your account balance to your bank account.

Stripe — Stripe offers easy payment processing integration with your website. Customers would visit your website, add a product to their shopping cart, start to checkout, and then Stripe would take over. They perform the back end processing for your online credit card transaction. Their fee is 2.9% + $0.30 per transaction, and money is automatically deposited in your bank account on a 2-day rolling basis. In addition, Stripe offers subscription billing if you want to set up recurring billing for customers.

Authoize.net — Like Stripe and PayPal, Authorize.net offers payment processing via your website. Their fee is 2.9% + $0.30 per transaction, but their setup is more complicated. They charge a $49 setup fee and a $25 monthly gateway fee. However, they offer additional fraud protection tools so if you are selling a more expensive product Authorize.net is a good option to consider.

Hiring Contractors

Are you dependent on others to operate your business? For example, you might need delivery drivers or class instructors or even IT professionals to run your business. Unless you need a certified professional and don't have that certification yourself, consider operating the business yourself until the workload becomes unmanageable. If you do hire someone, hire them as a 1099 contractor. This is a tax designation specifying that the individual is an independent contractor who provides a service to your business. This is a less expensive option since you won't have to pay employment taxes or provide other benefits that are obligatory for W-2 (full-time) employees. As your business starts to grow, you will want to hire employees (covered in Chapter 11).

Insurance

As your business starts to make sales, you should consider purchasing general liability (GL) insurance for your startup. This will protect your company's assets in the events of lawsuits and claims. The average cost of GL insurance is $500–$1,000 annually, which may seem expensive, but it can save you a fortune down the road. If you have a service business, some organizations will require that you have insurance before hiring you. Search online to compare quotes from insurers offering GL insurance.

Trademarks, Patents, and Copyrights

Do you need to trademark?

Trademarks are a way to protect your product name or logo from being used by another individual or company. Trademarks can cost a few thousand dollars however, and you should consider waiting to obtain a trademark until your business gets some serious traction. In the early days, your cash has more value elsewhere. Once you get serious traction, then you may consider securing a trademark for your product.

Do you need to file a patent?

A patent protects you in case someone else steals your product, invention, or design. According to the U.S. Patent and Trademark Office, the invention must be novel, have utility, and cannot be obvious to a person of ordinary skill in that particular art. Patents cost thousands of dollars and can take 3–5 years before they are issued. Once again, consider waiting before you submit a patent request. Most patents are worthless as only 2%–3% of patented products ever make it to market, and only 1% actually make a profit[2]. Also, patent claims are very specific so it's not that difficult for someone to design a legally similar product.

Do you need to secure a copyright?

Copyrights apply to creative works such as books, movies, art, and software. Copyright protection is created the moment your work is fixed in a tangible form, e.g., a saved file of your writing, a video, a sound recording, etc. Registering your copyright with the U.S. Copyright Office isn't a requirement for copyright protection. However, there are

---

[2] https://www.entrepreneur.com/article/80088

several benefits to registering your copyright, which costs less than $50. First, it makes it easier to assert your rights. Second, it allows you to send Cease and Desist letters. Third, it gives you the right to sue for infringement. Fourth, it entitles you to receive more money in case you win an infringement lawsuit.

Bookkeeping and Taxes

As you start to make purchases and receive revenue, you will need to perform bookkeeping. Bookkeeping is the recording of financial transactions in your business. One of the initial decisions you will have to make is whether to use the cash basis of accounting or accrual basis of accounting.

Under the cash basis, you record transactions on the date when the payment is actually exchanged. Under the accrual basis, you record transactions on the date the transaction happens regardless of whether you were paid yet. Let's say you sold and delivered a product to a customer in January, but they didn't pay for the product until February. Under the cash basis, you would record the revenue in February (when the customer actually paid you). Under the accrual basis, you would record the revenue in January (when you sold the product). Most small businesses choose the cash method since it simplifies bookkeeping and is easier to track cash flow.

Once you have decided on an accounting method, it's time to start recording transactions. By this point, you will have already made several purchases (i.e. website domain, email, legal entity formation fee) so you want to keep track of expenses. Initially you can use a simple spreadsheet. Create two tabs — one for revenue and one for expenses. On the revenue tab, record each sale using the date, customer, and amount. On the expenses tab, list the date, name of expense, and amount. As you make business purchases, record them as expenses. Make sure to rigorously maintain this spreadsheet. It maintains the corporate veil. (Your company is a separate legal entity and your personal assets can't be touched in cases of lawsuits, claims, and bankruptcies). In addition, it makes tax time easier, as all your business records will be in one place. You can use the data from your revenue and expenses to glean insights for better decision making. Eventually as your business grows and gets more complicated, you can transition to QuickBooks or other accounting software for small businesses.

Sales Tax
Before you open for business, make sure you

determine the correct percentage sales tax to charge customers. Sales tax can be imposed at the state, county, and city level, and varies based on where you live and what type of business you own. Reach out to your State's Department of Revenue to learn about the required sales tax for your customers.

Payroll Tax

If you have employees (not contractors), you will have to file several payroll forms on a quarterly and annual basis (IRS forms 940, 941, and 944). If you use contractors, you need to file a 1099 form for each contractor at the end of the year (if the total of their payments is above $600). All the large national banks (Chase, Bank of America, Wells Fargo, etc.) have online portals where you can schedule payments from your business bank account to employees/contractors. These banks also keep track of your payments for tax time and can file tax forms as required by law.

Tax Returns

As April starts to approach and you begin to fill out your taxes, there are a few considerations to remember. If you formed an LLC or an S corporation, your income or loss will flow directly to your individual tax return. If you formed a C corporation, you will have to file a corporate tax return in addition to your individual tax return. For preparing and filing taxes, you can hire a professional or do it yourself using an online service such as TurboTax. If your business is not very complex and you are comfortable with tax returns, consider using TurboTax. It's easy to use, reasonably priced, allows you to create/send 1099s, and walks you through every deduction. Otherwise, search online for a tax professional specializing in your company's industry and type of legal entity (LLC, Corporation, etc.). Look for an experienced accountant and compare reviews and rates.

Deductions
You will want to reduce your taxable income as much as possible by taking deductions. The IRS allows you to deduct startup and organizational costs on your tax return. You can deduct $5,000 in business startup costs and $5,000 in organizational costs, but only if your total startup costs are $50,000 or less. Business startup costs include purchasing a laptop, office supplies, website creation/hosting, advertising, etc. Organizational costs include the cost of forming an LLC/corporation and legal fees. According to the IRS, in order to be in business you need to have sales. You don't have to show a profit but you do need to have

revenue. Other tax deductible expenses that business owners can write off include company-related travel, meals and entertainment, and home office. Make sure to hold on to receipts for at least four years in the unlikely event that the IRS audits you.

Post-Year Analysis

After you finalize your revenue and expense numbers for the year, analyze them. For expenses, examine them and see where you can save money. Perhaps you can cut costs by changing your cell phone plan or buying shipping materials in bulk. Analyze your revenue for any trends. Perhaps 80% of your business comes from a select few customers. In the next year you could focus more on these customers and try to sign on other customers like them. There are many ratios you can use to analyze your data but perhaps the simplest is your profit margin. The formula for this calculation is:

$$\frac{\text{Total Revenue} - \text{Total Cost}}{\text{Total Revenue}}$$

Using this ratio, you will know what percentage of each sale you make is profit. You can compare your profit margin from the current year to previous years to analyze positive or negative trends. You can compare your profit margin to competitors in the industry and see how you stack up.

Chapter 8: Build your Website

A website is a must for every business. You can either create one yourself or hire a developer.

Building a Website Yourself

If your business is selling products online, consider creating your storefront using Shopify or BigCommerce. Both of these companies allow you to easily build an online storefront and process credit/debit card payments. There are hundreds of tutorials online to guide you through the creation process.

If you have a service business (or want more customization than Shopify and BigCommerce offer), you could create a website using a website builder. Some of you may be intimidated by the thought of building your own website. Trust me, it's not hard. The website builders nowadays are extremely easy to use, and you will get the hang of it within a few hours. They offer drag and drop creation interfaces, and the pricing is inexpensive. There are many website builders, each with its own benefits and drawbacks. Here are the four most popular:

	Wix	Weebly	Squarespace	WordPress
Offers Free Plan?	Yes	Yes	No, offers 14 day trial	Yes
Templates	500+	100+	60+	300+
Customer Support	Email, phone	Email, phone, chat	Email, chat	Depends on level purchased: Beginner(forums), Premium(email), Business(chat)
Perfect for:	General small business websites	Less tech-savvy entrepreneurs	Designers, photographers, online shops, restaurants	Any size business, blogs, those looking for more customization

	Wix	Weebly	Squarespace	WordPress
Pros	Easy to use, offers 250+ apps to customize your site	Easy to use, quick way to create a site	Modern and sleek templates	Offers the most customization with thousands of plugins available
Cons	Unable to transfer your content to a new template (you would have to create a new site)	Limited customization, templates not as good as others	More expensive, limited customization due to no plugins	More complicated to learn

Start by looking through the templates available on each website builder. Each template will include all the essential features of a website—menu, contact form, email signup forms, social media links, etc. Once you find a template you like, sign up for a free account with that website builder and start playing around with the features. Within a few hours, you will have a sense of whether that builder meets your needs. If you have questions, each builder provides voluminous support forums and there are countless YouTube videos you can refer to for help. Once you have built your website, you will want to pay for a monthly plan at your builder in order to remove their ads and link your own domain.

Using a Developer to build your Complex Website/App

If you are planning on building a complex website or mobile app but don't have technical expertise, you will need help from a professional developer. Often, good developers are expensive, but if you find someone you gel with, consider offering them equity in your business in exchange for their development work. If you can't find a tech co-founder, then you will have to pay a developer. It's easy to find companies online that offer app and website development services at inexpensive rates, but these firms are often located in distant foreign countries. You may find that language barriers and time zone differences impair communication and make working with offshore developers difficult. You need to be able to provide direct feedback for changes and ensure that your feedback is understood by the developer. Using a local developer is ideal so you can meet and review changes. There are several ways you can go about finding a freelance developer in your area:

A) Reach out to your friends to see if they know any good developers.

B) Engage in tech events in your community to network and find developers.

C) Create a job posting for a freelance developer. You can use post developer jobs on www.findbacon.com or www.jobs.github.com/positions

D) Contact local web or app development firms. You can search online for companies.

E) Find a developer using a freelancer platform. Some sites are:
   - Toptal.com
   - Upwork.com
   - Gun.io
   - Guru.com

Before signing on with any developer, make sure they provide clear estimates of total cost and timeline to completion. Do not pay them by the hour but instead when they reach project milestones and show you the corresponding progress. I once worked with a developer who insisted on being paid hourly to create a mobile app. The development work was supposed to take 2 months. After 2 months, the app was unfinished, and I had already paid the developer a substantial amount of money. I became less of a priority for him, and received a semi-functional version of the app 6 months later. Insist to pay by project milestones. Below is an example of payment milestones you can use for your development project, but know that every project is different. Depending on how much work is involved in each milestone, your percentage of payment may vary.

UI Design (Wireframes and Artwork) — 10%
Front-end Development — 20%
Back-end Development — 40%
Testing — 20%
Release — 10%

Chapter 9: Grow Online Presence

To build a robust online presence, you will want to perform Search Engine Optimization (SEO) and create social media pages to connect with your customers.

Search Engine Optimization

After building your website, perform SEO so customers can more easily find your company online. The goal of SEO is to have your business rank higher in customers' search engine results. There's a significant advantage in appearing on the first page of Google search results.

Here are steps you can take to improve your SEO:

1. Submit your website to search engines (Google, Bing) using the links below. Google.com/webmasters/tools/submit-url?continue=/addurl Bing.com/toolbox/submit-site-url

2. Create a Google My Business page, and once you have customers, ask them to leave reviews.

3. Reach out to other websites, bloggers, and publications to write about your business and link to your website. The more relevant links you have to your website, the higher your search ranking will be.

4. Create unique page titles for each page of your website.

5. Do not add meta keywords since Google ignores them and Bing flags them as spam.

6. Create a unique description (metadata) for each page of your website in the SEO settings on your website builder.

7. Write a paragraph describing your business and include keywords that potential visitors would use to find your website. Place this paragraph on the bottom of your homepage. It should not reappear on other pages of your website.

8. Create unique alt text for each image on your website. Alt text is a description of an image on a webpage. By writing alt

text for each image, search engines can better index your image.

9. Ensure you have the right header tags for text on each page (H1, H2, H3, H4, H5, H6). Header tags distinguish headings and subheadings on your website and run from H1–H6. The most important is H1 and the least important is H6. Header tags help search engine crawlers grasp the main topics of your content.

10. Create seasonal pages to take advantage of holidays (e.g. Christmas Sale or Fourth-of-July Service Special).

11. Create a custom 404 error page. A 404 error page can appear when a user clicks on a broken link or if a previously bookmarked page doesn't exist anymore. By creating a custom 404 error page, you can easily redirect users to your site.

12. Create a sitemap for your website and submit your sitemap.xml to Google Search Console. A sitemap is a hierarchical model of the pages within a website.

Google's Tools

Since Google owns 77% of the daily search engine volume[3], it's important to leverage their tools to maximize your placement in their search results. The most important tools are Google My Business, Google Analytics, Google Search Console, and Google AdWords.

Google My Business provides you with a free business listing which appears in Google Maps and Google Search. Create your free listing at www.google.com/business and once you have customers, encourage them to write reviews on Google My Business.

Google Analytics tracks who comes to your website, how they found your website, and what they do on your website. To set up your free account, visit www.analytics.google.com. Analytics will generate a unique tracking code which you can easily attach to your website through your website builder. Once Google starts to collect data, you will be able to see:

- Audience (who is coming to your website). By leveraging the Audience

---

[3] http://www.smartinsights.com/search-engine-marketing/search-engine-statistics/

view, you can see several helpful data points for your website including:

- o Visitor trends over time periods, e.g., this month vs. last month
- o How many of your visitors are new vs. returning
- o Your bounce rate, which is the percentage of visitors to your website who leave your site after only viewing one page
- o Demographics and interests of your visitors

- Acquisition (how people are finding your website). The Acquisition view is very useful because you can see how users are finding your website. Are they finding it through a direct Google search? Are they being referred from another website (perhaps one of your partners)? Are they reaching it from clicking on one of your social media posts? Are they clicking on one of your ads and being directed to your site? Through these metrics, you can see what's working and what you need to improve. For example, if you are getting most of your visitors through social media, then keep on pushing social media and even step up your efforts. If hardly any visitors are coming through Google search results, you need to improve your SEO.

- Behavior (where users are spending time on your website). With the Behavior view, you can see where users are spending the most time on your site. Let's say you realize that no users are reaching the products page on your site. You should place links to the products page more prominently on your homepage. Let's say the tool shows that users are spending only a few seconds on your services page; this could be a flag that you need to improve the content and layout of that page.

- Goals (set a goal and track its success). The Goals tool measures how well your site achieves an objective. An example goal could be a purchase or a sign-up (i.e., a user enters their email address). Let's say you start spending money for online ads. With the Conversion tool, you could track how effective those ads are by analyzing how many ad clicks result in the goal being achieved (product purchase or sign-up).

Google Search Console helps you monitor and maintain your site's presence in Google search results. Submit your sitemap at www.google.com/webmasters/tools. You can use this tool to see what errors your website is producing and what HTML improvements you can make. Perhaps your website is running slowly or loading improperly on mobile devices. The log might show that your image sizes are too large, and therefore you should reduce the file size of your images.

Google AdWords allows you to create and run ads to direct visitors to your website. If you want to jumpstart visitors finding your site, you should run ads on Google AdWords. After creating different ads, you need to add relevant keywords that users will type into Google to find your product or service. Google charges for ads using cost-per-click (CPC). Every time a user clicks on your ad, you will be charged. You would set a maximum CPC and a daily budget, and once your charges hit that budget, the ad would stop running until the next day when your balance resets. Your actual CPC depends on several factors including keyword bids from other advertisers, expected click-through rate, and ad relevance. Here are some tips to help you succeed with an AdWords campaign:

- Have ads link to the exact page you are advertising.
- Add negative keywords. Negative keywords are search terms you want Google to exclude. For example, let's say you add "free" as a negative keyword on your campaign; AdWords would not show your ad for any search containing the term "free".
- If your business is local, add your city's name before keywords.
- Use ad extensions since they can improve your click-through rate. Extensions add useful business data below your ad such as locations, prices, and phone number.
- Track conversions. By creating different ads, you can measure which ones lead to more conversions (customer signups, purchases, phone calls, etc.).

Go to www.adwords.google.com to get started. For support, there are hundreds of AdWords tutorials online.

Social Media

After creating and optimizing your website, create social media pages. There are many social media platforms today so we will only focus on a few—Instagram, Twitter, Facebook, and YouTube. Posting on social media can be time-consuming so you need to test which platforms are the most effective for your business and focus on those. To start, pick out two or three platforms and post a few times a week on each account.

Instagram—Create an Instagram account for your business. Grow your followers by adding engaging photos and videos pertaining to your business three times a week.

Twitter—Create a Twitter account for your business. Grow your followers by posting links, photos, and interesting content related to your business.

Facebook—Create a Facebook page for your business. Add a gallery of photos and list your business information for the public to see. Post engaging content and invite your friends to *like* the page.

YouTube—Create a YouTube channel for your business and post videos. There are several types of videos you can create. Your video could be a promo, or it could be an interview with an industry expert. It could be an instructive video, or it could be a funny video. For example, Blendtec, a company that sells blenders, has created a series of "Will It Blend?" videos. These funny, engaging videos show the founder blending iPhones and other items in one of their Blendtec blenders. Depending on how much you spend on the production quality of your videos, YouTube can be an expensive platform on which to post.

Tip #1: If you are posting on several platforms per week, use Hootsuite to manage your posts. Hootsuite is an online platform that lets you write posts in advance and automatically posts for you when you want. This tool will save you a great deal of time.

Tip #2: In order to build the "Hollywood set" and lend credence to your business, you can pay for followers in each platform using Fiverr. Now, don't load up each of your social media accounts with tens of thousands of followers. However, 1000 followers on each account would be fine. It will cost you $5 per thousand follows on each platform.

Chapter 10: Launch your Company

Your website and social media are live. It's time to launch! First, focus on getting press. Then launch your marketing efforts.

Press

Press is the best form of marketing because it's generally free. You have an exciting startup and you may find journalists eager to cover your story.

1. Make a list of publications, newspapers, news outlets, blogs, websites, etc. that you want to contact.

2. Search online for email addresses of the writers, section editors, and bloggers.

3. Write a pitch email. This is a 1–2 paragraph email describing the launch of your business that serves to entice a reader. Writers receive dozens of pitches every day so try to make yours stand out.

4. Send a customized individual email to each PR contact on the list you've created.

5. If you don't receive any responses, don't lose hope. Keep on trying and follow up every few weeks with those who haven't responded. You can also offer a free sample of your product/service to your press contact/blogger. For example, if your business sells unique skin care products, offer samples to writers. If your business provides walking tours, offer a free walking tour to your press contacts.

6. In addition to sending out individual press pitch emails, you can also push a press release online. First, write a press release outlining the launch of your business and its unique attributes. You can find many strong examples of press releases online. Then, create an account at PRLog.org and use their service to blast a free press release. You can use a paid service to reach even more publications. For example, PRweb.com and PRLog.com both have paid options that cost $150–$300.

Marketing

Every business is unique so you will need to try several marketing methods to see which combination works best for your business. Regardless of which marketing efforts you choose to pursue, you should first create a marketing plan. This plan will provide you with structure so you aren't arbitrarily throwing money around. It will also ensure you stay on top of your initiatives and help you determine what's working and what's not. Your marketing plan should include:

- Customer definition – Who is your customer? Are they male or female? Are they a tourist or local? Where do they live? How old are they? What is their socioeconomic status? This is the most important thing you need to figure out. Based on your customers' demographic, determine the best way to directly market to them without wasting time or money. For example, if you are going after millennials, Facebook and Snapchat ads might be your most effective medium. If you are going after tourists, then perhaps consider approaching hotel concierges about a partnership. Are you selling to consumers (B2C) or businesses (B2B)?

Taking a step back and thinking about your company, could you sell to both consumers and businesses? Perhaps with a few tweaks, you could sell to the other sector. For example, one of my businesses was a discount coupon app for NYC venues (restaurants, museums, retail, etc.). I marketed the app directly to consumers, but also to corporations as a corporate benefit they could provide to their employees.

- Competitor research – If you have competitors, how are they marketing their business? What is working for them? Emulate and improve upon what they are doing.

- Budget – How much money do you have in your marketing budget? Initially, you will want to spend more on marketing since you are a new company. However, as you may be bootstrapping your company, you need to be smart about where you spend your money. You want the most bang for the buck. As a comparison, established companies typically spend 10% of their sales on marketing.

- Marketing initiatives – You will want to list all the marketing initiatives you are going to undertake, along with their timelines and associated budget. Here are some marketing initiatives to get you started.

Marketing Initiatives
A) Advertising

- Online: Where do your customers spend their time? Do they use certain websites? What interests do they have? You have many options for online advertising:
  - Search engine ads (Google, Bing)
  - Social media ads (Facebook, Instagram, Snapchat, Twitter, YouTube)
  - Targeted websites ads (For example, if you offer a golfing-related service, you should reach out to online golfing forums about advertising on their site.)
- Offline: Do your customers live in a certain area? Do they read certain magazines? There are a plethora of offline advertising options:
  - Public transportation ads
  - Billboard ads
  - Newspaper ads

- o Magazine ads
- o Radio ads
- o Sponsorships
- o Free promotional items such as pens, mugs, bags, and t-shirts (check out Vistaprint.com)
- o Flyers and postcards — One of the cheapest advertising options is printing 500 flyers or 3x5 postcards and handing them out to potential customers.
- Remember to make your advertising campaigns unique. If you want your message to stand out, try to think of new ways to connect with your audience in places that are unexpected. You want to create catchy ad headlines that clearly state the benefit that your product/service offers. Consider using a copywriter and graphic designer to create compelling ads for your audience.

B) Email Marketing
- As you begin to receive inquiries, collect email addresses to create an email database that you can use to send out updates, news, and promotions. For example, you can blast out an email to your list every few months offering 10% off with a promo code.

- Use www.mailchimp.com to manage your email contact database and send out professional emails. The cost is free if you have less than 2,000 email addresses. If you have more than that, they offer pricing tiers based on the number of subscribers.

C) Partnerships — What other businesses are targeting your same customer demographic? Consider partnerships with those businesses. Be creative. Here are some example types of partnerships you can consider:

- Sell your service or product through partners. Have other businesses list it on their site and market it. In return, you pay them a commission for each sale (anywhere from 3%–15%). I offer my trolley on other bus charter sites. When they book a charter for me, I pay them a 15% commission.
- Co-marketing arrangement — Offer to create a cross-promotional email with another company. You email your customer list and your partner would email their customer list introducing each other's products. I did this with Hooch, a company that offers a subscription for a drink a day. I sent an email to my customers introducing

Hooch, and Hooch emailed their customers about my trolley company.

- Creative — Get creative with your partnerships. I partnered with Grouper (a group dating app) to offer an ultimate Grouper date on our trolley. Grouper users submitted entries to the contest using a unique Twitter hashtag, and at the end of the week, 6 Groupers won the date. Thousands of Grouper's users found out about my business, and my only cost was a two hour trolley ride.

D) Promotions — You can also entice customers to make a purchase by offering promotions. Here are some examples:

- Hold competitions. For example, you could run a contest on Facebook where potential customers are entered into a raffle to win a free service/product from your business if they tag five Facebook friends in a post about the business.
- Send out a survey email to customers offering them a discount if they answer the survey. Survey questions could include: how did you find out about our business, how would you market our business, what can we do to improve our business. Leverage your customers' suggestions to improve your business.

- When people visit your website, have a pop-up appear for new visitors that offers 10% off if they sign up for newsletters with their email address. This is a great way to build your email database with prospective customers.
- Use a third party vendor such as Gilt or Urban Daddy Perks. They have extensive subscriber lists they can use to promote your product. Bear in mind they discount the price of your product and then take a cut which significantly reduces your profit margin. Stay away from Groupon and LivingSocial as they often require you to discount your product to the point where you are losing money. In addition, their subscribers typically will not be repeat customers as they are looking for one-time cheap deals. For example, let's say you run a deal on Groupon selling your unique mascara. Your retail price to customers is $10. Groupon will offer your product to their user base for $5. Of that $5, you will receive $2.50 and Groupon will receive $2.50. You will only receive 25% of your retail price. It's a losing proposition. The more exclusive third party vendors such as Gilt and Urban Daddy Perks generally have

better terms for businesses. They will discount your product 20% and you keep 75% of the sale price. Using the same $10 mascara example, they would promote it to their user base for $8, and you would receive $6 from every sale. Consider using these vendors to spread awareness of your business.

E) Referral Programs — Referrals can be a great source for new customers. You are turning your customer base into advocates and lead generators for your business. The easiest method is to send an individual email to each customer thanking them for their business and asking them to refer their friends. You could also offer incentives. For example, you could email your customers saying that if they refer a friend who books your service or buys your product, they would receive a 15%-off coupon. Or you could offer a double-sided referral where you say "If your friend buys our product, we will give you 15% off and give your friend 15% off."

F) Reviews
- Reviews are important. Positive customer reviews validate and promote trust in your business to potential customers. For example, let's say you

are looking at purchasing a product and there are two options available. One option has no reviews, and the other option has great reviews. Which would you pick? Also, having reviews improves your SEO.

- Ask customers to leave reviews on relevant websites that offer reviews such as Google My Business, Yelp, TripAdvisor, etc.
- As a small business, even one negative review can be detrimental to your business. If you receive a bad review, do something to make it right. You could offer a partial refund or a discount off a future purchase. Perhaps the customer with the negative experience will remove their review. If this isn't feasible, respond to the negative review. Keep your response polite, professional, and apologetic.

G) Post on Social Media—Social media allows you to show a personal side behind the corporate curtain. It is an excellent way to connect with your audience. Engage your audience with questions, polls, videos, and interesting content. You want to keep it fresh by posting content regularly.

H) Continuously Improve SEO and your Website

- Use Google Analytics to determine how users are finding and using your website. Continuously make SEO improvements so you appear higher in search results. Getting other websites to link to your website will boost your search engine ranking.

- If you find that you have a high bounce rate on your website (average bounce rate varies based on the type of business), consider doing A/B testing using Unbounce. A/B testing is where you create two versions of a webpage and then over time, see which page yields better conversions.

- Add live chat functionality to your website. It offers customers the convenience of having their questions answered immediately and builds their confidence during the shopping experience. It benefits you by improving your conversion rate and average order value. LivePerson and Pure Chat are two of the many live chat companies providing this functionality at reasonable pricing.

I) Start a Blog—Blogs are a great way to boost SEO and create a personality behind your business. You can add a free blog to your website through your website builder or use WordPress. With blogs, you will want to create engaging content for your users. Blogs can be time-consuming so make sure you set aside time to post at least once a week.

J) Additional Sales Channels for Products

- Amazon—Consider selling your products on Amazon as well as your own website. More than half of U.S. online customers begin their product searches on Amazon[4]. Apply to be an Amazon seller and you will be able to list your products on their site. You will have two options: either fulfill orders yourself (when you ship your products to customers after each sale) or initially ship some of your inventory to Amazon and they will fulfill your orders for you. The former has the benefit of a lower commission from Amazon. The latter has higher commissions, but you don't have to store as much inventory, and

---

[4] https://www.bloomberg.com/news/articles/2016-09-27/more-than-50-of-shoppers-turn-first-to-amazon-in-product-search

customers are more likely to purchase your product as it will be Prime Eligible.

- Retailers and Distributors — If you solely sell your product online and want to expand to other sales channels, contact retailers and distributors to stock your product. Use the email template I showed you in Chapter 3 and follow up with phone calls.

K) Events — You can attend trade shows and networking events for your business. For example, if you sell a service for brides, you should research bridal shows in your area. If you sell niche clothing, you could attend trade shows for your niche.

L) Throw a Launch Party — Don't do this. It is a waste of money. Instead, email your friends and family letting them know you launched your own business and to help spread the word. Nothing may come of this email initially, but down the road, someone may ask your friend if they know of any company offering a particular product/service and they will think of your business.

Tip: You want to measure the effectiveness of your marketing efforts. The easiest way to achieve this is by asking customers how they found out about you. If customers purchased a product from you, ask how they found you when you email them the shipping confirmation. If you have a service business, you could include a field in your customer contact form that asks how they found you. Keep track of responses since you want to see which efforts are paying off. You want to know if your customers are finding you through a simple Google search or a Facebook ad or word of mouth. Based on your analysis, you can allocate more money to whichever effort is yielding the most customers.

Chapter 11: Scale the Business

You've been in business for some time. You're making a profit. Your business is growing. How can you scale your business so it grows more quickly and efficiently?

Introduce new products or services to your existing customer base

If you have a product business, expand your product line. Are there complementary products you can offer? Perhaps your company creates high-end water bottles. Consider expanding into sports bottles and travel mugs. You can cross-sell your new products to your current customers.

If you have a service business, consider adding a product component. Service businesses tend to be labor intensive. By "productizing" your service business, you can scale more easily. Products require less labor and have higher margins. For example, you can offer packages or a subscription. The latter has the benefit of creating a recurring revenue stream. For example, let's say you have a sales force and marketing consulting firm. You have realized that most of your customers are having the same set of problems—salesforce sizing and optimizing marketing spend. You hire a development team to create software that will automate these solutions and then sell that product to your customers. Or let's say your business offers training services, and you give lectures across the country. You can record yourself giving lectures and then sell those content segments as a package or subscription to customers.

If you manufacture domestically, consider using an international manufacturer

To reduce your cost per product, look at manufacturing your product overseas. Refer back to Chapter 7 for details on how to source an international manufacturer. Make sure you do your homework before switching vendors. You want to ensure that your products will still be of the same quality. Keep in mind the potential for negative brand implications/publicity for not using domestic workers.

Automate and delegate

You've been running your business on your own and the daily tasks are starting to suffocate you. It's time to start looking at ways you can automate your business. Here are some tools you can use:

DocuSign—send out contracts, receive signatures and payments online
Salesforce—automate your lead tracking and nurturing (CRM)
QuickBooks—simplify your accounting
Zendesk—customer service automation
Hootsuite—manage all your social media accounts on one platform
MailChimp—manage your email database and send out professional-looking emails

Besides leveraging tools, entrepreneurs should delegate tasks to further automate their business. For example, you can outsource your social media posting and customer service. Searching online, I've found social media consultants who will post on multiple platforms three times per week for a few hundred dollars a month. If responding to customer service emails is taking up most of your time, you should first update your FAQ on the website to answer more questions received in customer inquiries. Then, you should consider hiring someone to answer emails. That person could be a recent college graduate, a freelancer, or even a stay-at-home parent. Delegation can be hard for entrepreneurs as they naturally want to do everything themselves. It involves letting go of control over the business and trusting others to do a good job. However, by delegating the more menial tasks, entrepreneurs can focus on the more important tasks of growing the business.

Hire employees

As your business grows, you will need to hire full-time employees. Your first hires are the most important for your company. You want motivated, passionate individuals who will help set the pace and culture for your company. Start by creating job descriptions of the roles you would like to fill. To source applicants, first tap into your personal and professional network. If that fails, post jobs on LinkedIn and Indeed. It's free to post on Indeed, but LinkedIn will charge you based on job type and location. Once you have received several strong resumes, you can start to interview candidates. Here are some basic interview questions to ask every applicant, with subsequent questions tailored to your business:

Why do you want to work at our company?
Why is this role perfect for you?
What is your work style?
What are your strengths/weaknesses?
What are some ideas you have for the company?

Where do you see the company in five years and how can you help us get there?

Seek additional funding — venture capital

Your business is flourishing. Your numbers are trending up each month. You're growing quickly, but you need additional funding. Now is the time to approach venture capital firms. First, you need to determine which firms invest in your industry. Some VCs focus on healthcare, some focus on mobile technology, etc. Then, for each firm you want to determine the appropriate contact person. Once you find a good prospect with interest in the right area, visit LinkedIn and see if you have any mutual connections. The best way to get in contact with a VC is through an introduction by a friend. If you don't have any mutual connections, that's fine; it just means that your introduction email will need to be that much better. Below are several of the top VC firms to start your search.

A16z.com
Khoslaventures.com
Svangel.com
Accel.com
Nea.com
Sequoiacap.com
Firstround.com

Sparkcapital.com
Kpcb.com
Lsvp.com
Generalcatalyst.com
Greylock.com

Once you have a list of firms you are going to contact, you will need a pitch deck. You will want to create a PowerPoint that includes the following slides at baseline:

1. Introduction
2. Market Opportunity — What is the total market size and where do you fit?
3. Problem — What is the problem your business solves?
4. Solution — What solution do you provide?
5. Revenue Model — How does your business make money?
6. Customer/User — Who are they and how many? How will you acquire them?
7. Growth Strategy and Timeline — What is your vision and plans to get there?
8. Competition — Who do you compete against?
9. Management Team — What are the credentials of the management team?

10. Financial Projections — What is your current revenue/expenses and forecast?
11. The Ask — How much are you raising?

Once you have completed the pitch deck, you can start emailing venture capital firms with a few sentences about your business. Once you have their interest, send them your pitch deck. Make sure your deck is professional and eye-catching. Keep your deck to 15 slides or less. Spend a good amount of time creating the Management Team slide as this is one of the most important focus areas for potential investors. Highlight why your team is the best for this opportunity. If investors like your pitch deck, they will ask you to come in for a meeting. Make sure you are well prepared to answer all of their questions. If you have a technology platform, make sure you show them a demo. Your goal is to get them asking for more.

Closing

Congratulations! You have learned all the steps you need to start your own business. Use this formula to help you succeed.

Start by analyzing your lifestyle and how much risk you are comfortable with. Begin generating ideas through observation of everyday life and brainstorming sessions. Once you have several ideas, start testing them out to see if consumers or businesses will use your service/product. This is critical and will save you from making the mistake of investing money and time in a business that doesn't work.

Once you have found your winning idea, further define what it is, who you're selling it to, and how you're selling it. This will serve as a high-level strategy for your company. Now you can structure your company. Determine a name, buy a domain, create an LLC, and open a business bank account. You have several options when it comes to funding your company so make sure to leverage the different options available before asking friends and family for money.

In today's business world, an online presence

is of paramount importance so you need to create a professional-looking website and social media pages for your business. When you have completed these steps, you can watch your work come to fruition. Launch the business. Seek press. Launch marketing efforts. Get your name out there. As you progress, keep track of your revenue and expenses. As your business gains traction and grows, you can consider scaling mechanisms such as productizing, automating, and seeking additional funding.

Along the way, don't be afraid to reach out to other entrepreneurs for support and guidance. If you are encountering obstacles, it's likely that someone they know has experienced similar problems in the past. Most communities have entrepreneur meetup groups so you can network with other entrepreneurs.

Time passes fast. You may be thinking about an idea and then it's five years later. The onus is on you to execute. You will never be completely within your comfort zone as you launch your first startup, so stop hesitating. Don't spend your life in a cubicle working for someone else. Don't make excuses about timing or waiting until next year. You don't

want to lose your idea to someone else.
Starting is the toughest part but once you
begin, prepare to be energized and excited. I
wish you the best of luck on the journey ahead.

Appendix A: Entrepreneur Interviews

Learning from other entrepreneurs is one of the secrets to success. I've interviewed several entrepreneurs to find out the tips and advice they have for aspiring founders.

Peter Weitz, founder of Greenstone Partners

Peter started Greenstone Partners, a commercial real estate company, in 2010. Today, he has 30 employees and manages over $100M in assets. His company focuses on three businesses: leasing/brokerage/management, investments, and construction.

How did you get the idea for your business? How did you start the company?

I always had a desire to be in real estate so I started working in the industry. After two years of working for a commercial brokerage, I left since I wasn't making any money. I gave up and took a job with a large bank. About three months into the new job, I received a call from my old boss who told me that this investor kept calling him and asking for me. My old boss had explained I didn't work there anymore, but this investor was still adamant about speaking with me. Getting his contact info, I called this investor with the intention of telling him I didn't do real estate anymore.

Once on the phone with him, he said he would only work with me and wanted to buy a building. I ended up representing him on a building purchase, and since then have never looked back.

What is your favorite aspect of being an entrepreneur?

I love being able to actualize an idea. I can look at a building, see the potential of what it can be, and fix it up. Real estate is not a zero-sum game. Instead of carving up a pie into pieces, you can grow the pie.

What would you say are the top skills needed to be a successful entrepreneur?

Network like crazy, love your business, be confident, and believe in yourself. You cannot be an entrepreneur unless you have a belief of "why not me?"

What lessons have you learned on your path as an entrepreneur?

I learned that the clichés are right. Be accountable. Be honest. Surround yourself with good people. Attitude is everything. It's important to hire people that are coachable and have the right attitudes.

What advice do you have for aspiring entrepreneurs?

1) Just do it. People overthink and over plan. They delay their actions and hide behind planning. Now is the time to start. If you think about it and keep thinking about it, you're delaying it. Let's say you have to cold call someone; people spend all this time doing research when they should just pick up the phone and call. Today is the day.

2) Manage your relationships and your reputation.

Drew Lakatos, founder of Active Protective

Drew founded Active Protective in 2012. His company has developed a belt for the elderly that can accurately determine human falls and deploy an airbag around the hips to protect the wearer.

How did you get the idea for your business? How did you start the company?

I'm a startup guy. This is my third startup. My first startup crashed in the tech collapse. My second startup did okay, but was not a windfall. So I decided to go back to the corporate world and wait for the next idea. Fast forward to 2005, and I'm attending a hospital Christmas party with my wife, a trauma PA. She introduces me to one of the trauma surgeons, Bob. While chatting with Bob, a Level 1 trauma page comes in, and my wife has to leave to help out. The patient was an 87-year-old woman who had been hosting a Christmas dinner party. She had fallen down a staircase and broken her hip. Speaking more with Bob, a former combat casualty surgeon, I learned that many of the traumas coming into suburban emergency rooms weren't gunshots and knife wounds like in the cities, but elderly people falling and dying. He said that the 87-year-old patient that my wife just left for had a 3% chance of surviving based on injuries he assessed from his pager. He shared an idea to create a belt that could inflate to protect the hips in the event of a fall. As this was 2005, the technology wasn't there yet. We filed patents and waited for the technology to mature. It wasn't until 2012 with the advent of cold airbags and the price reduction of 3D motion sensors that the business became a reality. I quit my job and began working on Active Protective full-time.

What is your favorite aspect of being an entrepreneur?

I love doing something no one else thought was possible. I love creating something from nothing. That is the biggest rush for me. This product has the potential to help people on a global scale. We may one day save more lives in a month than car airbags save in a year.

What would you say are the top skills needed to be a successful entrepreneur?

I would say agility, willpower, and being well-rounded. You need to be able to quickly connect with others on a meaningful level— whether it's an investor or a tech person. Another skill needed is scrappiness. Before I was funded or even had a prototype, I attracted the attention of the U.S. Department of Veteran Affairs (VA). They invited me to their mobility lab to test my product. I had to quickly build a prototype from scratch. Using the inner tube of my mountain bike tire and air bag materials I sourced from scrap cars at a junkyard, I created a prototype which the VA determined was more effective than elderly hip pads currently on the market. Sometimes you just need to get scrappy.

What lessons have you learned on your path as an entrepreneur?

The toughest part about being an entrepreneur is that you have to pursue something long before the rest of the world thinks it makes any sense. You need willpower and perseverance. You need to be sane enough to execute and pursue something before it's in a rational phase.

What advice do you have for aspiring entrepreneurs?

1) The rejection can be suffocating at times. Stay positive.

2) Have an unbreakable will. You will have to make sacrifices, people may not care what you're doing, and you will have to overcome countless obstacles all for a slim chance of success.

Alexandra and Thomas Pericak, founders of COnut Butter

COnut Butter, founded in 2015 by Alexandra and her husband Thomas, is a New Orleans-based nut butter company producing blends of whole roasted nuts and organic cold-pressed coconut oil.

How did you get the idea for your business? How did you start the company?

Alexandra: I've always had a passion for healthy food and lifestyle. Thomas has type 1 diabetes, and I have food intolerances so I was always experimenting in the kitchen. Throughout my 20s, I had jobs in finance and also worked with nonprofits, but I was never passionate about them. I went back to school for nutrition, and on the side starting doing research and working with healthy recipes. Realizing the benefits of coconut oil, I started incorporating it into my recipes including my nut butter. I couldn't keep up with the demand at home since Thomas and I were eating all of it. I started selling my coconut oil-infused nut butters at farmers markets in Denver. It began as a side hustle and quickly became my main passion. I couldn't wait to get home and try new recipes. At this time, Thomas received a job opportunity in New Orleans, so we relocated. It's then that I started approaching grocery stores. Currently, we are in 30 stores in the state of Louisiana and growing every week. Our products are all self-distributed. We do all the blending, packing, marketing, sales, and stocking in the stores.

Thomas: We started on a small scale going direct to consumer. Then we expanded our retail focus to regional grocery chains. Now we are talking with co-packers to expand our production. In terms of health food, New Orleans is 10 years behind compared to other cities. It's cool being a pioneer in the health space in New Orleans. If we had stayed in Denver, I don't know if we would have been as successful starting out since there is so much competition there.

What is your favorite aspect of being an entrepreneur?
Alexandra: Making your own rules and being able to work with my spouse. It's amazing to work with someone you trust so deeply who can celebrate all the wins as much as you.

What would you say are the top skills needed to be a successful entrepreneur?
Alexandra: Being a self-starter, staying motivated, and being passionate. There is no one to give you a gold star or hold you

accountable except yourself. Stay positive and don't accept "no" for an answer.

What lessons have you learned on your path as an entrepreneur?

Alexandra: Stay authentic. It's so easy to compare yourself to other businesses. You look around and see what others are doing or what ingredients they're using and wonder if you should do the same. I have to continually remind myself to stay authentic. Also, I've had to desensitize myself to hearing the word "no". You're going to hear "no" sometimes.

Thomas: Yes, you will hear some "no's." However when one door closes, another opens. We've learned to stick with our instincts. I remember going back and forth about the name of our product. There were so many names we could go with, but in the end we went with our gut and it worked out.

What advice do you have for aspiring entrepreneurs?

Thomas: Be realistic. Be smart in your planning and be realistic in your expectations. Then pull back your expectations even more. Start slow, make sales, and build a book of business.

Alexandra: Get outside of your comfort zone.

Every conversation you have is an opportunity to boost your knowledge. Never turn down opportunities to meet new people. Put yourself out there. Make yourself uncomfortable.

Stephen Corby, founder of Specless

Specless, founded by Stephen in 2012, is a platform for publishers to bring the market unique and differentiated premium advertising experiences.

How did you get the idea for your business? How did you start the company?

In 2012, I was working for a large publisher. Working as their mobile advertising specialist, my job was to figure out what ad products we were going to bring to market as mobile traffic in the industry was growing dramatically. While we did a great job selling during that period, execution-wise, the campaigns were a mess. Companies weren't giving us their ad creatives in all the different sizes we needed, especially for mobile phones. I wanted to create a solution so ads could be resized automatically and rendered to different sizes. So I left the firm and started Specless.

What is your favorite aspect of being an entrepreneur?

Control. I love being able to control my own destiny. Right now, I'm in a situation where I get to collaborate with lots of people, but ultimately can make my own call on any aspect of the business. I've always been confident in my ideas and felt that unless I had the freedom to pursue them, I wouldn't get a chance at those ideas.

What would you say are the top skills needed to be a successful entrepreneur?

1) Having a very clear vision. You need to paint a vivid picture and visualize what your business looks like, what you're selling, who are your customers, where will you be in five years, etc. From my perspective, there are two types of successful entrepreneurs — those who have a vision, become obsessed with it, and go after it, and those who try a bunch of stuff and see what works. For better or worse, I'm the former.

2) Perseverance. In the early stages where there isn't much going on, being able to show up and do something every day, day in and day out, is very hard. You have to become obsessed with getting to your goal. It's a weird level of obsession that not everyone has. Especially as the CEO of a startup, your job is to make sure the company doesn't run out of money and lives to fight another day.

3) Flexibility. You will have to work with different people of different mindsets who may have conflicting views. Make sure you have a willingness to compromise.

4) Being even-keeled. Don't let your emotional pendulum swing too much.

5) Ability to learn. I couldn't express some of the ideas I had to developers so I learned to code myself.

What lessons have you learned on your path as an entrepreneur?

1) Don't get ahead of yourself. Fail quickly. If your business is creating a tech product to fix a problem, don't go too far down the path before getting it into users' hands and trying to sell it. We completely over-engineered the product before we had any customers. We thought we would build the perfect product and everyone would want it. We tried selling to ad agencies, but it turned out that they liked resizing ads for clients since they charge hourly. We came to the realization that all the inbound requests we were receiving came from publishers (companies selling ads). The publishers wanted a way to differentiate their direct sales by offering different ad sizes to advertisers. We ultimately figured out our product/market fit.

2) When things get really busy, there's a tendency to work in your business vs. on your business. You can get pulled into the weeds instead of focusing on broader goals and sales. If I put in an hour of work, I need to make sure that hour of work pushes me towards my goals.

3) A common mistake early on, especially for

startups, is to model all your goals around fundraising. I would look at what venture capital firms care about and model my goals to fit that need. These days, you don't need money to scale unless you have a very unconventional business model. There's a huge tendency to think you need a bunch of money or you won't be able to succeed. Try to figure out how you can scale without a massive amount of VC funding. By doing that, you're going to maintain ownership and not dilute yourself.

What advice do you have for aspiring entrepreneurs?

Just go do it. Don't half ass it. Whatever you want to do, go out and do it. Focus on long-term goals and break those down into smaller goals that you can achieve. Entrepreneurs have a tendency to focus on goals and not use KPIs (Key Performance Indicators) to measure them. If you want to hit $1M in sales, what is the first micro-step to get there? Don't get lost at the 40,000 foot high-level view of the business. Break it down. What are you doing today? What's going to get you there—calls, meetings? How many do you have scheduled in the next 30 days? Sales isn't a great KPI, but rather look at what can you affect (for example, how many calls you can make). Don't get overwhelmed by big goals. Break them down into micro steps.

Appendix B: Failing

Sometimes after all your hard work and perseverance, your venture might not work out. It might fail. Don't beat yourself up. It stings but it will get better. I've had at least twice as many failures as successes. But for every failure, I've gained priceless knowledge and insight which has helped me in my next venture. The key is to persevere and remain motivated. One of my first ventures was an online social network allowing high school and college students to connect. The company was called Collegetacts, and it was a colossal flop after 3 months. My biggest issue was that I couldn't find the right mix of incentives to attract users to the site. However, out of this experience, I learned two important lessons: First, I learned how to build a website using an online web design platform. Second, I learned how to tap into the power of a personal network. In order to secure initial users on the site, I reached out to all my contacts via email, Facebook, and phone calls urging them to join the site and support my business. Despite my initial fears of failing and looking like a fool, I took a chance which initially paid off as I secured my first 100 users to the site within a few days.

For another venture, I looked to build a platform allowing video gamers to compete and wager against each other. Although seeing big potential for the business, the venture flamed out after five months. First, my tech co-founder wasn't able to devote enough time to development. Second, the regulatory environment was changing. Wagering and online gaming was increasingly coming under government scrutiny which ultimately hastened our decision to shutter the business. From this experience, I learned the importance of choosing a business partner who is fully committed to the business. If their heart is not in it, it is time to let them go. Friends and/or family may not be the best choice for business partners, and as other entrepreneurs can tell you, it can be a source of headaches (and potential ending of relationships) down the road. I also learned the importance of proper regulatory/licensing research before launching your business. Make sure you understand the current regulatory environment facing your venture and have a sense of where the industry is heading.

I was able to leverage these lessons in my next venture—importing clothing from Italy, retailing it online, and distributing it across the world. Using the skills gained from previous failed ventures, I was able to design the website quickly, spread the word to my social networks efficiently, and choose the right business partner to ensure the future success of the company. Initially, I tried everything from online ads to posters to visiting stores with samples. It was haphazard and ineffective. Over time, I learned that I needed a marketing plan to organize my efforts, waste less money, and analyze the effectiveness of my campaigns. Create your marketing plan before your business is launched. Analyze your efforts to determine the most effective forms of marketing (e.g., online, print, billboard, TV, special events, etc.) as well as your target customer segments. This will help move the needle to ensure you have sales coming in the door on Day 1.

Always keep learning and incorporating lessons learned from your experiences. Do not get discouraged when a venture fails. Never give up and remember—your next successful venture may be just around the corner!

Appendix C: Helpful Links

Business Advice and Mentorship
Score.org

Consumer Testing
Surveymonkey.com
Google.com/forms
Unbounce.com
Landerapp.com
Ebay.com
Etsy.com

Crowdfunding
Kickstarter.com
Indiegogo.com

Online Storefront Builders
Shopify.com
Bigcommerce.com

Domain Name Search
Instantdomainsearch.com

LLC Formation Services
Legalzoom.com
Corpnet.com
Mycorporation.com
Bizfilings.com
Rocketlawyer.com

Employer Identification Number (EIN) Application
Irs.gov/businesses/small-businesses-self-employed/apply-for-an-employer-identification-number-ein-online

Business Credit Card Comparison
Creditcards.com/business.php

Business Logo Creation
Freelogodesign.org
Fiverr.com
99designs.com

Business Cards Printers
Vistaprint.com
Moo.com
48hourprint.com
123print.com
Eliteflyers.com

Federal Small Business Grants
www.grants.gov —
comprehensive database of grants
administered by various government agencies

www.business.usa.gov —
uses a questionnaire to help you find relevant
grants

www.sbir.gov/sbirsearch/solicitation/current
— grants for technology innovation and
scientific research

www.challenge.gov —
lists government grant competitions

www.grantwatch.com —
lists grants for small businesses, nonprofits,
and individuals

State and Regional Small Business Grants
www.sba.gov/tools/local-assistance/sbdc —
provides you with a list of local Small Business
Development Centers that you can contact to
find grant opportunities

Corporate Small Business Grants
www.smallbusinessgrant.fedex.com —
FedEx small business grant up to $25,000

www.mltapthefuture.com —
live pitch competition for grants from$20,000-
$100,000

www.nase.org/become-a-member/grants-
and-scholarships/BusinessDevelopmentGrants
.aspx — offers monthly $4,000 grants

Specialty Small Business Grants
For Women —
www.entrepreneur.com/article/290807

For Veterans —
www.nerdwallet.com/blog/small-business/small-business-grants-for-veterans

For Minorities —
www.nerdwallet.com/blog/small-business/small-business-grants-minorities

Accelerators
Ycombinator.com
Angelpad.org
Techstars.com
Amplify.la
Startx.com
500.co
F6s.com/accelerators (search tool for accelerators)

Angel Investors
Angelcapitalassociation.org/directory
Gust.com
Angel.co
Startupangels.com
Allianceofangels.com
Goldenseeds.com/angel-network

Coworking Spaces

Wework.com
Regus.com
Impacthub.net
Galvanize.com
Techspace.com
Industriousoffice.com
Theyard.com

Domestic Manufacturers

Kompass.com
Makersrow.com
Thomasnet.com

International Manufacturers

Alibaba.com
Indiamart.com
Bambify.com
Globalsources.com
Kompass.com

Auction Sites

Liquidation.com
Palletbid.com
Techliquidators.com
Gsaauctions.gov
Govsales.gov

Order Fulfillment Companies (for Storing and Shipping Inventory)
Amazon.com/sell
Shipwire.com

Home Shipping Services
Stamps.com
Shipworks.com
Shippingeasy.com

Payment Processors
Paypal.com
Stripe.com
Squareup.com
Authorize.net

Website Builders
Wix.com
Squarespace.com
Weebly.com
Wordpress.com

Searching for Freelance Developers
Findbacon.com
Jobs.github.com/positions
Toptal.com
Upwork.com
Gun.io
Guru.com

Submitting Website to Search Engines
Google.com/webmasters/tools/submit-url?continue=/addurl
Bing.com/toolbox/submit-site-url

Google Tools
Google.com/voice
Analytics.google.com
Google.com/business
Google.com/webmasters/tools
Adwords.google.com

Press Release Services
Prweb.com
Prlog.com

Productivity Tools
Mailchimp.com
Quickbooks.intuit.com
Docusign.com
Salesforce.com
Zendesk.com
Hootsuite.com

Venture Capital Firms
A16z.com
Khoslaventures.com
Svangel.com
Accel.com
Nea.com

Sequoiacap.com
Firstround.com
Sparkcapital.com
Kpcb.com
Lsvp.com
Generalcatalyst.com
Greylock.com

Secretary of State Information
Alabama
http://sos.alabama.gov/
334-242-7200

Alaska
https://www.commerce.alaska.gov/web/
907-465-2530

Arizona
https://www.azsos.gov/
602-542-3230

Arkansas
http://www.sos.arkansas.gov/Pages/default.
aspx
501-682-1010

California
http://www.sos.ca.gov/
916-653-3795

Colorado
http://www.sos.state.co.us/
303-894-2251

Connecticut
http://portal.ct.gov/sots
203-566-3216

Delaware
http://www.corp.delaware.gov/
302-739-4111

District of Columbia
https://os.dc.gov/
202-727-7278

Florida
http://dos.myflorida.com/
904-488-9000

Georgia
http://sos.ga.gov/
404-656-2817

Hawaii
http://ltgov.hawaii.gov/
808-586-2727

Idaho
https://sos.idaho.gov/
208-334-2300

Illinois
http://www.cyberdriveillinois.com/
217-782-7880

Indiana
http://www.in.gov/sos/
317-232-6576

Iowa
https://sos.iowa.gov/
515-281-5204

Kansas
http://www.kssos.org/
913-296-2236

Kentucky
https://www.sos.ky.gov/Pages/default.aspx
502-564-2848

Louisiana
https://www.sos.la.gov/Pages/default.aspx
504-925-4704

Maine
http://www.state.me.us/sos/
207-287-3676

Maryland
http://www.sos.state.md.us/Pages/default.as
px
410-225-1330

Massachusetts
http://www.sec.state.ma.us/
617-727-9640

Michigan
http://www.michigan.gov/sos
517-334-6206

Minnesota
http://www.sos.state.mn.us/
612-296-2803

Mississippi
http://www.sos.ms.gov/Pages/default.aspx
601-359-1333

Missouri
https://www.sos.mo.gov/
314-751-1310

Montana
http://sos.mt.gov/
406-444-3665

Nebraska
http://www.sos.ne.gov/dyindex.html
402-471-4079

Nevada
http://nvsos.gov/sos
702-687-5203

New Hampshire
http://sos.nh.gov/
603-271-3242

New Jersey
http://www.state.nj.us/state/
609-530-6400

New Mexico
http://www.sos.state.nm.us/
505-827-4508

New York
https://www.dos.ny.gov/
518-474-4752

North Carolina
http://www.sosnc.gov
919-733-4201

North Dakota
http://sos.nd.gov/
701-328-4284

Ohio
https://www.sos.state.oh.us/
614-466-3910

Oklahoma
https://www.sos.ok.gov/
405-521-3911

Oregon
http://sos.oregon.gov/Pages/index.aspx
503-986-2200

Pennsylvania
http://www.dos.pa.gov/Pages/default.aspx
717-787-1057

Rhode Island
http://sos.ri.gov/
401-277-2357

South Carolina
http://www.scsos.com/
803-734-2158

South Dakota
https://sdsos.gov/
605-773-4845

Tennessee
https://sos.tn.gov/
615-741-2286

Texas
http://www.sos.state.tx.us/
512-463-5555

Utah
https://corporations.utah.gov/
801-530-4849

Vermont
https://www.sec.state.vt.us/
802-828-2386

Virginia
http://www.scc.virginia.gov/clk/index.aspx
804-371-9141

Washington
https://www.sos.wa.gov/
360-725-0377

West Virginia
http://sos.wv.gov/Pages/default.aspx
304-558-8000

Wisconsin
http://www.sos.state.wi.us/
608-266-3590

Wyoming
http://soswy.state.wy.us/
307-777-7311

Index

ABOUT THE AUTHOR

David Pike is a serial entrepreneur with 10+ ventures spanning multiple industries. He has been featured in Forbes, The New York Times, New York Post, Huffington Post, Business Insider, and VentureBeat among other publications. David is a mentor and advisor for startups at Founder Institute, and his writing has been published in Investment Advisor and Under30CEO. He has guest lectured on entrepreneurship at his alma mater, the University of Michigan, where he graduated with a BSE in Industrial Engineering.